WHY JUSTICE FAILS

BY WHITNEY NORTH SEYMOUR, JR.

Why Justice Fails
The Young Die Quietly:
  The Narcotics Problem in America
Small Urban Spaces (editor)

WHY JUSTICE FAILS

WHITNEY NORTH SEYMOUR, Jr.

WILLIAM MORROW & COMPANY, INC.
NEW YORK • 1973

THIS book is affectionately dedicated to my father, for whom elevation of the standards of the legal profession and attainment of justice have been the goals of a lifetime.

Acknowledgments

THIS book would not have been possible without the patience and good humor of two indefatigable ladies, Agnes Marquette and Reta Thompson, proprietors of the Sequel Secretarial Service in Lakeville, Connecticut, who typed and retyped the manuscript with gusto and reformers' zeal. I also acknowledge my deep indebtedness to my friend and colleague James W. Rayhill, who gave up his free time to review the manuscript and make a number of excellent suggestions; to Hillel Black, my editor at William Morrow & Company, who thought up the idea for the book in the first place; to Elizabeth Otis, my charming literary agent, who encouraged me to believe that I could write for popular publication; to my many-talented secretary, Hester B. Coe, who lived through the legal struggles that generated many of the ideas expressed here; and above all, to my wife, Catryna, and our daughters, Tryntje and Gabriel, whose enthusiasm and support despite many lost weekends was one more contribution to the full and happy life we have had together.

Finally, I record my gratitude to the spirit of those reformers over the years—past, present and future—who believe that the lawyer's duty is to speak up about things that need correcting. As Oliver Wendell Holmes once wrote: "Law is the business to which my life is devoted, and I should show less than devotion if I did not do what in me lies to improve it."

W.N.S., Jr.

Man can tolerate many shortcomings of his existence, but history teaches us that great societies have foundered for want of an adequate system of justice—and by that I mean justice in its broadest sense.

—CHIEF JUSTICE WARREN E. BURGER
Speaking at the National Conference on the Judiciary
Williamsburg, Virginia, March 12, 1971

Contents

CONTENTS

Introduction

Whose Responsibility Is Justice?

Two youths are arrested in a small Southern town while trying to break into a gas station. A third boy, waiting in the car which the three had stolen a few days before, makes his escape. He burglarizes several other gas stations before being arrested in another state. All three boys have similar backgrounds and no previous convictions. The first two boys, prosecuted in one state, each receive a three-year prison term. The third boy, prosecuted in a different state, is placed on probation.

A low-income family in a large metropolitan center purchases a television set on a time-payment plan. Shortly after the set arrives, the picture tube stops working. The husband complains to the store, and after several weeks of unfulfilled promises on their part to repair the set, he stops payment. A few weeks later he is told by his employer that a garnishment order has been placed against his wages, and he is discharged. It is his first notice that a law suit had been filed against him for nonpayment and the first he learned that judgment had been entered on default.

The mother of a nineteen-year-old boy serving a four-year prison sentence for stealing a $116 welfare check from a hallway mailbox reads in the morning newspaper that a corporate executive has been convicted of evading $60,000 in income taxes and received a suspended sentence.

A traveling salesman takes his car to a service station for repairs. The service-station attendant places the car on a hydraulic lift rack, raises it up, and then lowers the rack again after discovering that he does not have the proper parts to make the repairs. The salesman, busy reading a parts manual, is standing near the rack as it descends. The attendant does not warn the customer and the descending rack lands on his right foot and crushes it. The salesman is hospitalized and unable to work for several months. A trial jury subsequently returns a verdict in his favor against the gasoline company that operates the station, but the trial judge sets the verdict aside on the ground that as a matter of law the salesman was guilty of contributory negligence for standing near the rack, and therefore cannot recover anything for his injury.

A thirty-one-year-old man climbs through a ground-floor window into a woman's bedroom in a residential community one morning at 4 A.M., steals the sleeping woman's purse and creeps out again. Neighbors witness the episode and call the police. Two patrolmen respond and apprehend the suspect as he is walking away from the scene. The man pulls out a pistol and aims it at one of the officers. The gun misfires. The suspect is arrested for attempted murder and unlawful possession of a dangerous weapon. Upon arraignment, he is sent to a state mental institution for psychiatric observation. Two months later an indictment is filed against him, but no one informs the hospital. A few weeks afterward the man is released from the institution. Five months later he is arrested again, charged with killing a fifteen-year-old girl by reaching through a ground-floor bedroom window and stabbing her with a knife as she lay sleeping. The police say that the man is a prime suspect in three similar killings and a series of other attacks that have terrorized the neighborhood since his release.

These composite cases are typical of wrongs which can and do occur in our court system almost every day. They are also symptoms of a larger problem which has gone on for too long— public neglect of the way our courts work.

This book is about injustice—the injustice actually *created* within our established legal system. Frequently that legal system works extremely well, achieving fair results at reasonable cost. But often it fails. When this happens people usually blame the lawyers and judges. In the words of today's teenagers, that is a cop-out. Some lawyers and judges may indeed fail to do all they can to right wrongs, and some may actually commit unethical and illegal acts—but lawyers and judges alone are not responsible for injustice in our legal system. The responsibility belongs to all of us.

As a lawyer I recognize that this book deals with a sensitive subject. Many attorneys and judges will react defensively and be critical of the fact that I have dealt primarily with the negative side of the administration of justice. That is a risk I am willing to take because of the importance of the subject and the need for it to be discussed openly and frankly. My examples of injustice are not intended as sweeping generalizations, but are meant only to point up faults that need correcting.

The failure of justice in our legal system should not be blamed on any one individual or group of individuals. It is the result of no one's assuming the responsibility for seeing that justice is fully done. Much injustice derives from lack of interest, lack of concern and lack of knowledge. Neglect is a far more serious problem than we have been willing to admit. Apathy pervades many parts of our society, but is nowhere more destructive than in the administration of justice.

Yet a strong legal system is necessary to the future of America. The fair settlement of private disputes, the evenheaded enforcement of the law, and the sensible and sensitive handling of antisocial conduct are all essential to people's living together in peace.

This book has been organized to explore the various major problem areas in the administration of justice. It looks at the role of lawyers and judges, the status of the poor in the courts, society's attempts to deal with crime and the correction of offenders, and the relationship of the courts to juvenile problems, to the individual and to such substantive areas of legal dispute as automobile accidents and business affairs. One chapter dis-

cusses the unfulfilled role of the media in achieving a better system of justice in America. A final one attempts an overview of
the total problem of why justice fails. I intend this not as an
exposé, but rather as an attempt to raise and explore the problems that interfere with the workings of a fundamentally sound
concept, so that we can get about the business of correcting them.

By "we" I do not mean members of the legal profession alone.
The achievement of justice is the job not only of lawyers and
judges but also of the media, public officials, community leaders,
academicians and, above all, the general citizenry. Justice is
like liberty, and its existence depends on the moral determination of all people that there shall be no injustice. In the words
of Learned Hand:

> Liberty lies in the hearts of men and women; when it dies
> there, no constitution, no law, no court can save it; no con-
> stitution, no law, no court can even do much to help it.

The same is true of justice.

Chapter 1

The American Legal System

Winston Churchill once wrote:

> Civilization means a society based upon the opinion of civilians. It means that violence, the rule of warriors and despotic chiefs, the conditions of camps and warfare, of riot and tyranny, give place to parliaments where laws are made, and independent courts of justice in which over long periods those laws are maintained.

The history of the American legal system has been a continuing struggle toward impartial and independent courts of justice. Although we have made remarkable progress, we have not yet reached the goal.

Because the original charters of the American colonies were granted by English kings, it was natural that the English judicial system should have been transplanted to American soil. Early Colonial laws followed those of England, and uniformity was assured because the appellate tribunal for Colonial judicial proceedings was the English Privy Council, of which the King himself was a member. Colonial governments did not distinguish carefully between the three branches—legislative, executive and judicial. Usually, the Governor and his council exercised general appellate jurisdiction. At the end of the seventeenth century, a Superior Court exercising both appellate and original jurisdiction was established in Massachusetts, with the right of direct appeal to the King in Council, in England. Similar courts came into being in other colonies: Pennsylvania, Rhode Island, Connecticut, Virginia and New Hampshire. By the time of the Revolution, there were two varieties of appellate courts: one similar to the House of Lords (made up of legislators), the other similar to the King's Bench (made up of judges). Usually appointed by the Governor, judges of the trial courts performed administrative functions in addition to hearing cases. It was not unusual to find a judge whose duties included assessing and levying taxes, licensing trades and appointing petty judicial officers.

After the American Revolution, the states reexamined their judicial structures and began to institute a system of checks and balances, which resulted in a separation of the judicial from the legislative and executive branches. In some states distrust of legislative power led to formal constitutional establishment of the courts. In others the legislatures were empowered to create at least the inferior courts. The whole evolution of judicial power in this country, however, has been toward greater independence from the other branches of government. The declaration by Chief Justice John Marshall, in *Marbury v. Madison*, that the Supreme Court could invalidate Acts of Congress which were in violation of the Constitution was probably the most important milestone on the road to judicial autonomy.

In very recent years, the self-direction of the courts has resulted in judges taking a more active role in dealing with social issues which formerly were regarded as the sole province of the executive and legislative branches. As citizen groups have felt frustrated by their inability to get legislators or executives to act on pressing current problems they have increasingly turned to the courts. Contrary to most people's expectations, the courts generally have responded in an affirmative and creative fashion. Various members of the judiciary—particularly in the Federal courts—applying a broad sense of justice and a belief in the positive use of judicial power for the public good, have grappled with deep social issues and designed important remedies.

There are obvious limitations on what courts can do, most notable of these being their inability to provide funds, but they can still go a long way toward forcing lazy public officials to do their duty, or preventing other officials from abusing the public's rights.

There are many things wrong with our court system. The dockets are crowded; cases are delayed unconscionably; and the whole process is too costly. But there are also some great things about it, and the greatest of all is its ability to produce results. A final court order is usually enforced. Whatever may be the difficulties along the way, that final order usually puts an end to uncertainty and forces the parties to comply with its mandate. As a result, we have tended to use our court system for far more than simply deciding private disputes and enforcing criminal law.

In the New Deal reform days it was assumed that most of society's ills could be solved by administrative bodies. We have learned the hard way that administrative agencies can be just as stultified as any court because, like the courts, they depend on the quality and energy of the people who make them run. If these people grow apathetic, the institutions grow ineffective and unresponsive to the social needs they were designed to serve. It has been natural, therefore, that as administrative agencies have grown increasingly bureaucratic, we have more and more turned to the courts to deal with problems which cannot be adequately handled by other agencies of government. Contrast the relative failure of the Federal Trade Commission against the success of the courts in countering anticompetitive practices over the past thirty years. Meeting each new challenge from the economic community, the courts developed ever more sophisticated applications of antitrust law: a series of court actions blocked concentrations of capital, price-fixing and other closed-door practices by giants of industry. The FTC, meanwhile, became so sluggish that it finally had to undergo major surgery. Whether that administrative agency will ever contribute significantly to the economic health of the nation still remains to be seen.

The courts have often shown imagination and fortitude in

dealing with contemporary problems. It was the court system that provided voting rights for disfranchised Southern blacks, brought about the reorganization of state legislatures on a one-man-one-vote basis and mandated school integration. Most recently, the court system launched the battle to protect our natural resources.

The fight to preserve our environment can be dated from a single court decision in the first *Scenic Hudson* case. In 1963, the U. S. Court of Appeals for the Second Circuit overruled the granting of a license by the Federal Power Commission that would have permitted Con Edison to cut the heart out of Storm King Mountain in the Hudson Highlands for the sake of a pumped storage power facility. That case was instituted by a small group of citizens who withstood vituperation from the utility's supporters, as well as the huge expenses of litigation, in order to fight for a principle. Since the original *Scenic Hudson* decision, many other groups have resorted to the courts in the battle to save the environment. So has the Federal Government. In a series of recent decisions, the U. S. district courts have forged weapons to combat the fouling of the nation's waterways. A series of Federal injunctions now prohibit the discharge of heavy metals, acids and other harmful effluents. This advance has been achieved through judicial interpretation and application of an 1899 statute—evidence of the courts' creative responsiveness to society's needs.

This activist approach on the part of the courts has spawned a new phenomenon: the public-interest law firm. At first, various citizen groups retained private counsel to help litigate some of the new social issues. Then the NAACP Legal Defense Fund was organized to concentrate legal resources in civil rights cases, particularly in the South. When people saw how effectively such concentrated resources could work, providing a machinery for both fund-raising and litigation, similar groups began to spring up. Now there are a substantial number of public-interest law firms in the country working full time on such matters as the environment and the rights of consumers, and undoubtedly more will emerge in the future.

There are many other areas of contemporary social policy where the courts will presumably be called upon increasingly for help, among them:

(1) Enforcement of statutes guaranteeing equal job opportunities for large segments of unemployed.

(2) Protection of consumers, particularly those with educational and economic handicaps, against oppression and overreaching on the part of creditors and collection agencies.

(3) Correction of inequities in welfare and poverty programs and funding.

(4) Assurance of health services to the poor under Medicare, Medicaid and other programs established for that purpose.

(5) Guarantees of proper implementation of publicly funded programs designed to help children in the public schools.

(6) Guarantees of equal access for all to decent housing, and elimination of practices which contribute to housing abuses by real estate speculators and to the soaring cost of new housing construction.

(7) Assurance that programs designed to provide nursing care and other services for the aged will be properly and fairly administered.

Many thoughtful people regard this expanding judicial activism with mixed feelings. As the courts have enlarged their own jurisdiction to deal with social problems that would otherwise be neglected, they have also added to the burden on the court system itself, with the result that it has become overloaded. Obviously this crowding of the court schedule is not just the result of volunteered increase of the work load, but derives from many other sources as well. President Nixon commented on the situation in an address to the National Conference on the Judiciary held in Williamsburg, Virginia, in 1971:

The nation has turned increasingly to the courts to cure deep-seated ills of our society—and the courts have responded; as a result, they have burdens unknown to the legal system a generation ago. In addition, the courts had to bear the brunt of the rise in crime—almost 150 percent over the past ten years, an explosion unparalleled in our history.

And now we see the courts being turned to, as they should be, to enter still more fields—from offenses against the environment to new facets of consumer protection and a fresh concern for small claimants. We know, too, that the court system has added to its own workload by enlarging the rights of the accused, providing more counsel in order to protect basic liberties.

Our courts are overloaded for the best of reasons: because our society found the courts willing—and partially able—to assume the burden of its gravest problems. Throughout a tumultuous generation, our system of justice has helped America improve itself; there is an urgent need now for America to help the courts improve our system of justice.

There are two major cornerstones to the American system of justice. One is trial by jury. Although occasionally jurors will reach quixotic results, by and large they employ a much more reliable standard of fairness and provide a surer protection of individual liberty than any known alternative. Individual judges can be subjected to pressures; juries usually cannot. The second cornerstone is the requirement that witnesses must testify in open court and be subject to cross-examination. No greater tool has been found to test the truth of a witness's testimony or the accuracy of his recollection than to have the lawyer for the opposing party ask prying questions to make sure that the witness is firm in his statements and accurate in his perception. The right of confrontation and cross-examination is not perfect by any manner of means, and too often is abused through witness intimidation or improper cross-examination, but it comes as close to producing the truth as any fact-finding technique known to man. If there is any flaw in our implementation of these key concepts, it is our tendency to rely more on procedure than on substance.

Some years ago, Judge Learned Hand drove Justice Oliver Wendell Holmes in a horse-drawn carriage to a session of the United States Supreme Court in Washington, D.C. As Judge Hand dropped Justice Holmes off in front of the Capitol Building, Hand said, "Well, sir, good-bye. Do justice." Mr. Justice

Holmes turned and scowled. "That is not my job," he said. "My job is to play the game according to the rules."

The emphasis in our courts on playing by the rules can itself lead to injustice. Gamesmanship replaces the quest for truth. A desire to win can replace a desire for the just outcome. The operation of the rules of the system needs to be studied and challenged constantly to make sure that the rules are producing justice. We do not have such a constant challenge and review, and we should.

The legal system in America today, however, is far more than a court structure and rules of court procedure. It extends over much of the government and private establishment in this country, from lawmakers, to lawyers, to judges, to litigants, to police, to correction officials and ultimately to the taxpayers who directly and indirectly foot the bill. The impact of the legal system touches the lives of most Americans one way or another, but it falls most heavily on those poor and lower middle income families who are caught up in criminal prosecutions, collection suits, and other enforcement proceedings without friends, resources or adequate legal representation. If we are ever to achieve justice under this system we must continuously examine all of its component parts and not merely tinker with technical rules and organization charts. Justice must be part of the basic fiber of the entire system and not merely an accidental chance by-product.

Chapter 2

Lawyers, the Courts and Justice

ON July 5, 1972, a Federal grand jury in New York City filed an indictment charging a Manhattan criminal lawyer, a city detective and a private investigator with conspiracy to obstruct justice. The grand jury contended that the three men had arranged for the theft of secret grand jury testimony and statements of prospective government witnesses in a pending case in which the lawyer and the investigator had been charged with subornation of perjury. All three were later convicted.

Three weeks later the same Federal grand jury indicted an assistant district attorney, a Queens defense lawyer and a bail bondsman for conspiracy to fix a criminal case before the county grand jury. The indictment alleged the payment of a $15,000 bribe through an undercover agent to bring about the dismissal of charges relating to the unlawful possession of two loaded pistols.

Two days later the grand jury indicted a Bronx defense attorney for attempting to bribe a New York City detective, Robert S. Leuci, to commit perjury in a criminal narcotics prosecution in the state Supreme Court. According to the indictment, the lawyer offered $20,000 to the undercover detective if he would give false testimony at the client's trial on charges of possessing heroin with intent to sell.

These cases raise serious basic questions about the legal profession:

How is it possible for persons who will engage in such perversions of justice to be licensed to practice law in the first place?

Why aren't the canons of ethics enforced more vigorously to prevent improper professional conduct before it reaches the stage of criminal corruption?

Attempts to answer these questions point up sharply the general inadequacy of traditional legal training, admission procedures and bar association grievance machinery to prevent dishonesty and incompetence in the practice of law. Such inadequacy in turn points up one of the major reasons why justice fails.

ADMISSION TO THE BAR

When Thomas Jefferson started out to study law in 1762, he had two choices. One was to go to London and enroll in one of the English Inns of Court. The other was to read law with an established attorney in the Colony of Virginia. He decided on the latter course, and entered the Williamsburg office of George Wythe, with whom he studied for five years. Jefferson rose at five in the morning and spent long hours abstracting everything he read. Law books were scarce. Prior to 1776 only thirty-three law books were printed in America, eight of them editions of the same work. Although there is no precise record of young Jefferson's schedule of studies, one may infer that it closely resembled the course of law studies he himself later outlined for a young friend: rising until 8:00 A.M., physical studies; 8:00 A.M. to noon, read law; noon to 1:00 P.M., read politics; in the afternoon, read history; dusk until bedtime, read belles-lettres, rhetoric and oratory. One of Jefferson's goals was to attain "the most valuable of all talents, that of never using two words where one will do."

Legal education in America has gone through a revolution since the eighteenth century. The practice of reading law in attorneys' offices has been replaced by formal instruction in three-year law school programs. Law school instruction has brought rigidity and isolation as students generally study stale facts and abstract principles, then argue moot cases removed from the real world of the law. One of the most unfortunate losses along the way has been Jefferson's economy of words. Lawyers are trained in an argot of their own. Verbosity is a badge of the trade.

Law school enrollments today are at an all-time high, with the number of students far exceeding the prospective job opportunities. Many students regard legal training not only as a gateway to a professional career but as an important training in its own right for other types of activity. For the 1971–72 school year there were 146 law schools accredited by the American Bar Association, with an enrollment of 94,468 students. The number of law schools has remained relatively static despite a sharp increase in enrollments. The result is substantial overcrowding.

Many criticisms have been aimed at present legal education. Law schools usually rely on appellate court decisions for teaching fact situations and legal interpretations. Although appellate court rulings reflect legal doctrine, they are only a small part of legal practice. Hence the frequent criticism that law schools omit the most important aspects of practicing law—fact gathering, negotiation and client relations. Other common criticisms center on the fact that schools also fail to deal with the all-important matter of administering a law practice (or a government or corporate law department), and largely concentrate on a trade school approach to matters of procedure and to the functioning of courts and administrative agencies; students are not taught *why* the system works the may it does and what might be done to improve it. Nor are they taught even the most basic skills in writing and public speaking so that they can clearly express ideas.

Law school interest in social problems has been largely disorganized and uncoordinated. Law professors tend to follow their particular hobbies while students organize their own work without much guidance. The schools make no comprehensive effort to explore the profound social forces which so significantly affect the practice of law and the administration of justice, including problems of housing, poverty, welfare, health services, education and ghetto culture. Law school training on such subjects as ethics and professional responsibility is also woefully inadequate.

There are also defects in the prevailing method of instruction in law schools, whereby students are grouped in classrooms to listen to a professor expound his notions. Many of the new teaching methods and materials that have exploded on university campuses, including computer technology, audiovisual techniques, field studies, peer teaching and others, have somehow bypassed the law schools. One notable exception has been the development of clinical programs in a number of law schools to permit students to work in the field with real problems. These programs have been made possible by the Council for Legal Education in Professional Responsibility, headed by Orison S. Marden and funded by the Ford Foundation. But on the whole, today's law school graduate is a long way from being a well-rounded lawyer, and, as a result, may never be one.

In the United States today a would-be lawyer needs simply to complete the required period of law school training, pass the bar examination of the appropriate state and be approved by the local "Character Committee." Although the Character Committee does have a certain *in terrorem* effect by requiring that the applicant file lengthy forms and affidavits or letters from employers and sponsors, a Character Committee rarely refuses an applicant his license to practice law. One of the most obvious reasons is that this committee does not function until *after* an applicant has completed his law studies and passed his bar examination. By that time he has invested at least three years of his life and thousands of dollars in his legal training; to turn him down on grounds as subjective as "character" would be almost unthinkable. The character committee procedure, therefore, is largely rubber-stamping. It will exclude convicted felons, but that is about all. In 1971, 2084 candidates applied for admission to the bar in New York State—only *one* was turned down.

Since there are no limitations on who can apply to law school in the first place, the net effect is that anybody who is willing to invest three years there is pretty well assured of being admitted to the bar, whatever his personality or character traits.

There were approximately 342,000 persons licensed to practice law in the United States as of 1971. About 70 per cent of these are in private practice, either as individual practitioners or as members of law firms. Another 15 per cent are employed by private corporations. The remaining 15 per cent are employed in public positions with Federal, state and local government. Some 17,922 new lawyers were admitted in 1970, an increase of 67 per cent over 1960. Many of the traditional employment opportunities for lawyers have reached the saturation point.

Despite the large increase in the number of law students and widened entry into the legal profession, minority representation has been extremely poor. Indeed, there are few areas of American life where minority groups have a smaller voice of their own. Today there are only 3,800 black lawyers in the country, just over 1 per cent of the total. The present law school enrollment includes only 2,400 blacks, about 2.5 per cent. If the black population were to have the same percentage of black lawyers as whites have white lawyers, the number of black attorneys would have to be increased tenfold. This drastic limitation on the black lawyer representation available for black citizens is particularly pronounced in the South. A recent article by a black graduate of New York University Law School, A. J. Cooper, gives the figures on page 13 as the ratio of black lawyers and judges to the black population in each of eleven Southern states.

Mr. Cooper himself returned to Alabama to practice law immediately after being admitted to the bar. He now lives in a county with a population of 112,959 blacks and only 4 black lawyers. In the southern half of the state there are between 300,000 and 400,000 blacks but only these same 4 black lawyers. The potential clientele of 75,000 to 100,000 blacks for each of these men contrasts sharply with the national average of 560 persons to each white lawyer. As a result, Mr. Cooper points out, white lawyers handle about 60 to 70 per cent of the

State	State Population	Whites	Blacks	White Lawyers	Black Lawyers	Black Judges
Alabama	3,444,165	2,528,983	908,247	3,245	46	1
Arkansas	1,923,295	1,561,108	357,225	1,954	15	0
Florida	6,789,443	5,711,411	1,049,578	10,828	89	2
Georgia	4,589,575	3,387,516	1,190,779	5,447	70	3
Louisiana	3,643,180	2,539,547	1,088,734	4,998	91	2
Mississippi	2,216,912	1,393,283	815,770	2,469	48	0
North Carolina	5,082,059	3,891,510	1,137,664	4,297	70	2
South Carolina	2,590,516	1,794,430	789,041	2,177	59	1
Tennessee	3,924,164	3,283,432	631,696	4,721	49	3
Texas	11,196,730	9,696,569	1,419,677	17,122	95	2
Virginia	4,648,494	3,757,478	865,388	6,298	103	3
TOTALS	50,048,533	39,545,267	10,253,799	63,556	735	19

black population's business. Mr. Cooper also notes that because of their position in the community, these white lawyers are rarely inclined to raise constitutional issues or provide aggressive representation for their black clients. Mr. Cooper is particularly critical of fellow black lawyers who have avoided practicing law in the South and instead have remained in more affluent centers like New York. He is bitter in his condemnation of black lawyers who content themselves with a few hours of volunteer work in urban ghettos as part of their big-city practice:

> It's easy to work uptown with a legal services office and go to the Village at night or to a Broadway play or to see Ike and Tina at the Garden. It's not very hard to pull down $16,000 a year at a firm, give the ghetto 5 or 10 hours a week (if that), pay $350 a month for a great apartment, eat lunch at French restaurants (on a client's account) and take vacations abroad. No doubt these lawyers are learning; the question is what are they learning, and for whom are they learning it?
>
> I guess the black community will have a lot of corporate mergers this year, with a similar amount of sale and leasebacks. What I don't have to guess about is that there are literally millions of blacks in the South whose property is being literally stolen from them with phony deeds, mortgage foreclosures and forged wills. What I do know is that millions of blacks are being deprived of their personal liberty

for alleged criminal offenses without the benefit of counsel or with some white counsel who simply doesn't give a damn.

The shortage of minority lawyers is not limited to the South. In New York City, for example, the black and Puerto Rican populations are 1,800,000 and 1,200,000 respectively. Black lawyers in New York total 400, a ratio of 1 for every 4,500 black residents. Puerto Rican lawyers number only 65, a ratio of 1 to 20,000.

PROFESSIONAL ETHICS

Abraham Lincoln personified the lawyer of compassion and high ethical standards. Those who knew him when he was a trial lawyer in Illinois spoke of his fairness, his concern for others, his integrity, his warmth and humor. Carl Sandburg tells of Lincoln's being retained to help another lawyer defend a man charged with the theft of a horse. When Lincoln arrived at the county jail with his co-counsel, he observed the client talking with his wife, who was obviously in poor health. When the client handed Lincoln ten dollars as a fee and said that it was all the money he had, Lincoln looked toward the woman and asked, "How about your wife? Won't she need this?" Lincoln then handed over half of his fee to the defendant's wife.

Abraham Lincoln articulated his principles in the following advice to members of the bar:

> Discourage litigation. Persuade your neighbors to compromise whenever you can. Point out to them how the nominal winner is often a real loser—in fees, expenses and waste of time. As a peacemaker, the lawyer has a superior opportunity of being a good man. Never stir up litigation. A worse man can scarcely be found than one who does this. Who can be more nearly a fiend than he who habitually overhauls the register of deeds in search of defects in titles, whereupon to stir up strife and put money in his pocket? A moral tone ought to be enforced in the profession which would drive such men out of it.

The "moral tone" of which Lincoln spoke has grown ever weaker with the passing years and the rapid expansion of the legal profession.

In a simpler day, the unwritten principles and noble ideals of the legal profession effectively governed its actions. Lawyers relied on the integrity of their colleagues to see to it that professional standards were maintained. It is significant that no formal national standards of professional ethics were adopted until 1908, when the American Bar Association approved the original thirty-two canons of professional ethics. The ABA Canons were based principally on a code of ethics adopted by the Alabama State Bar Association in 1887. Those in turn had been distilled from a series of lectures delivered by Judge George Sharswood under the title "Professional Ethics" and published in 1854. What a happy world it must have been in which men did not need to lay down a set of rules for professional conduct. But something was happening to the legal profession as the nation grew to maturity, and the need for rules became increasingly clear.

During the early days of the United States the need for attorneys was quite limited, and legal questions were relatively simple. Toward the end of the nineteenth century, however, dramatic changes began to take place, among them the population explosion, the rise of industrialization, and the increasing role of government. As these forces continued to operate through the second century of the nation's history, they had a profound effect on the role of lawyers. People crowded into the cities, the pressure of living together generated strife and the crime rate soared. In the fields of business and government the increasing complexity of legal relationships gave rise to new laws and regulations, as well as to new regulatory bodies, administrative agencies and private rules of conduct, each of which in turn increased the need for attorneys and made their job more complex. Disputes, laws and problems proliferated. Attorneys proliferated, too.

Gone are the days of the small-town practice. Most lawyers

have become specialists. Increasingly, they are detached from the other members of their own profession and the noble ideals which once were its cornerstone. The "leaders of the bar" are usually deeply committed to solving the problems of large corporations or other well-heeled clients whose legal problems command the best talent available. Such leading lawyers have little time for the problems of the criminal courts or the small-claims courts, which deal with the lives and aspirations of the poor.

The number of attorneys now practicing in large metropolitan areas is so great that they can assume there is little chance that they will ever run into the lawyer on the other side again. The result has been a deterioration in the spirit of goodwill and camaraderie, as lawyers have turned to fighting each other in order to gain advantage for their clients. It is commonplace today to hear lawyers in court accusing one another of the most shabby conduct—lying, cheating, deception. Many lawyers try to keep their adversaries off balance by utilizing tactics such as holding back copies of court papers until just before an argument begins, so that the opponent has no chance to read them. This same pettiness permeates many of the courts and their staffs as well. It is not at all unusual to hear a judge berating a lawyer, a court officer shouting, or a clerk refusing to answer a lawyer's question about some procedural step.

Most lawyers do not concern themselves with the difficulties that afflict the administration of justice, such as overcrowding of the courts, abuse of the disadvantaged and mishandling of criminal cases, because they have no direct involvement in these courtroom situations. Moreover, as the reputation of the legal profession has declined correspondingly, many attorneys have come to feel that there is little they can do to improve the overall integrity of their colleagues or the standards of judicial selection. Increasingly, lawyers concentrate entirely on their own special fields of interest and leave these problems to others, with the result that they go largely unattended.

In 1970, the American Bar Association restated the basic professional obligation of the lawyer:

Every lawyer owes a solemn duty to uphold the integrity and honor of his profession; to encourage respect for the law and for the courts and the judges thereof; to observe the Code of Professional Responsibility, to act as a member of a learned profession, one dedicated to public service; to cooperate with his brother lawyers in supporting the organized bar through the devoting of his time, efforts, and financial support as his professional standing and ability reasonably permit; to conduct himself so as to reflect credit on the legal profession and to inspire the confidence, respect, and trust of his clients and of the public; and to strive to avoid not only professional impropriety but also the appearance of impropriety.

In April, 1972, a committee appointed by the New Jersey Supreme Court reported a "diminishing concern for the integrity of the profession" among lawyers. The special nine-man committee found that many lawyers were reluctant to police the legal profession and report fellow lawyers to bar association committees for disciplinary action. The committee also concluded that the present system of handling complaints against lawyers is too slow. The committee report recommended establishing a centralized investigatory agency attached to the administrative office of the courts; enlisting the services of county detectives and state police to ensure that suspended or disbarred lawyers do not continue their law practice; and cracking down on fee-splitting and other improper means of soliciting of clients.

The Association of the Bar of the City of New York employs a full-time staff of experienced former prosecutors who investigate hundreds of complaints against lawyers each year, and produce a sizable number of disbarments, suspensions and censures. The depressing fact about the work of this committee is the extent of improper lawyer conduct it unearths. Although there is a certain amount of outright larceny, corruption or other unlawful conduct among lawyers, the most common violation of the relationship between lawyers and their clients is "neglect." Approximately 80 per cent of all clients' complaints against lawyers relate to the lawyer's failure to perform his professional responsibilities promptly or at all. Of course this discouraging picture reflects only those problems serious enough to come to the committee's attention, some six hundred per year, but it is symptomatic of the most common failings of mediocre lawyers— procrastination and indecision. In all of New York State, however, there were only 45 cases in which disciplinary sanctions were applied in fiscal year 1971, out of a total bar of 52,000. There were 21 disbarments (14 on consent), 15 suspensions and 9 censures.

What has been particularly troublesome has been the increasing number of criminal prosecutions against lawyers for violating the laws. Many of these violations, such as failure to file tax returns, do not result in any significant disciplinary action.

There has been a recent increase in malpractice suits against lawyers. Whereas in the past it was hard for a wronged client to find an attorney who would bring suit against a professional colleague, this inhibition no longer exists and the number of malpractice suits against lawyers is sharply on the rise. Of these malpractice claims, by far the largest single group, 45 per cent are based on "neglect." The biggest recoveries, running as high as one hundred thousand dollars, have resulted from the lawyer's failure to file legal papers on time, his allowing the statute of limitations to expire, time for appeal to run out, or other legal deadlines to pass.

Ideally, the profession should be able to police its own members. In England the legal profession regulates itself with no trouble at all, for the simple reason that admission to practice is controlled by the same machinery that controls the discipline of lawyers. Since the English bar is divided up into solicitors (who do the office work and deal directly with clients) and barristers (who only do courtroom work), it is much simpler to keep a firm control over courtroom conduct. English barristers are governed by a single professional entity made up of the four Inns of Court (tradition-laden institutions where barristers frequently have dinner together and supervise the education of candidates for admission to the bar) and a Senate of the four which coordinates educational and ethical standards and discipline.

The Inns of Court provide intensive training in standards of conduct and ensure their strict observance, so that disciplinary processes are rarely needed. In the United States, any one of the hundreds of thousands of lawyers admitted to the bar may handle a case in court, so that discipline by one's peers is virtually impossible. Moreover, the large number of law schools and the varying standards for admission, combined with the fact of fifty-one different licensing authorities and a proliferation of state and local bar associations, makes it equally impracticable to maintain uniformity in standards or approach.

Other European nations exercise close controls over courtroom conduct. In France, for example, the litigation bar includes 7,000 *avocats,* similar to English barristers; 1,500 *avoués,* a specialized group which files written briefs in court; and fewer than 30 *agréés,* who appear only before certain commercial tribunals. The positions of both the *avoués* and *agréés* are virtually hereditary, hedged in by tradition and protocol. Although there is at present a movement to merge these three sections of the trial bar, they nonetheless will continue to be completely separate from the office lawyers, called *notaires,* who handle property transactions, wills and marriage contracts, and the *fiduciaires,* who handle tax matters. Still another group exists in France, called the *conseillers juridiques,* who require no special training and provide legal advice to persons not involved in one of the areas already covered by the trained professionals. There is a strong movement in France to set up some form of regulation of these *conseillers juridiques* to ensure their adherence to a minimum standard of legal training and regulation.

The lack of disciplinary controls over courtroom lawyers in the United States has been a source of considerable concern to the legal profession. The committee which drafted the "Standards for Criminal Justice" for the American Bar Association has urged that state bar associations be strengthened as the enforcement agencies for professional standards. Chief Justice Burger, in an address before the American Law Institute in Washington on May 18, 1971, expressed particular concern about the misconduct by unruly lawyers in the courtroom. "When men shout and shriek or call names, we witness the end of rational thought process, if not the beginning of blows and combat."

Probably the heaviest blow against effective policing of the legal profession was dealt by the Supreme Court of the United States in its 1967 decision in *Spevack v. Klein*, 385 U.S. 511. In that case, a New York lawyer had been disbarred by the State courts for refusing to testify at a judicial inquiry into his professional conduct. The attorney had claimed his Fifth Amendment privilege, saying that his testimony would tend to incriminate him. The five-man majority of the Supreme Court ordered him reinstated. Justice Douglas, writing for four of the justices, said that a lawyer can as freely refuse to testify on grounds of self-incrimination as any other person suspected of a crime. Justice Fortas, who himself subsequently resigned from the Court because of questions raised as to his own integrity, joined the four to make up the majority, saying that a lawyer does not even have the same responsibility as a State employee to account for his actions, and therefore cannot be disbarred for refusing to explain his conduct.

In an eloquent dissent, the late Justice John Marshall Harlan spoke for all of those concerned with the decline in professional ethics:

> This decision, made in the name of the Constitution, permits a lawyer suspected of professional misconduct to thwart direct official inquiry of him without fear of disciplinary action. What is done today will be disheartening and frustrating to courts and bar associations throughout the country in their efforts to maintain high standards at the bar.

The *Spevack* decision was probably the capstone in the deterioration of professional standards. It clothed the dishonest lawyer with the rights of a defendant in a criminal proceeding, while leaving the disciplinary machinery with all of the weaknesses of a self-enforcement body. The obvious next step—a public prosecutorial staff with full criminal investigative capabilities to police lawyers—has not yet come about, but it may soon.

In June, 1970, a special committee of the American Bar Association headed by former Supreme Court Justice Tom C. Clark, at the conclusion of a three-year evaluation of disciplinary enforcement in the legal profession, reported the existence of "a scandalous situation that requires the immediate attention of the profession." Thereafter a number of state committees were established to review local enforcement procedures. One of these, in New York State, issued a detailed set of recommendations for sweeping changes in procedure in June, 1972, warning,

> There are indications of increasing public cynicism about the profession's capacity and will to keep its own house in order. If we do no more than ignore or attempt to explain away those indications, we should not be surprised to one day find an official-looking stranger scouring out the house with a detached and ruthless thoroughness.

But while the bar committees meet and discuss the problem, the problem itself continues to go on largely unchecked, leaving the principal policing function in the hands of the public prosecutor. It is not surprising, therefore, to read of the recent indictment of a former Assistant United States Attorney on charges of having stolen virtually all of the savings of one of his clients, an elderly widow who had entrusted him with the management of her entire inheritance of $219,560. When the thefts were finally discovered, the widow had only $48 left in her savings account. According to the indictment, the lawyer had withdrawn almost all the rest of the money for his own use. With the change in standards of admission and supervision of professional conduct, it may well be that only a full-fledged prosecutive arm is able to police lawyers who abuse their positions of trust for personal gain.

LAWYERS AND THE COURTS

The relationship of lawyers to courts is a two-way street. While the courts and the bar associations have failed to achieve comprehensive discipline of attorneys who violate standards of conduct, so attorneys themselves have failed to restrain or criticize misconduct by judges. Indeed, the legal profession has done a weak job at best in setting standards for the selection of judges and the administration of the courts. Although a handful of attorneys have espoused high judicial standards and sought reforms, most turn their backs on the whole process. The result has been the selection of many judges who are mediocre if not downright incompetent. Moreover, when judges fail to perform effectively, or engage in some form of misconduct, attorneys virtually never raise a voice in public criticism.

In a sense, lawyers have a built-in conflict of interest when it comes to selecting judges or being critical of their performance. In a more perfect world they might feel free to express criticism of judicial misconduct or incompetence, but most attorneys assume that if a lawyer should ever be heard to criticize a judge, other members of the court would take reprisals when the lawyer next appears to argue a case. Even the ethical standards under which an attorney must function tend to discourage public criticism of the courts. The oath of admission to the bar includes a pledge to "maintain the respect due to courts of justice and judicial officers." Although the Code of Professional Responsibility does urge attorneys to exercise their special obligation to aid in the selection of qualified judicial candidates, and to prevent political considerations from outweighing judicial fitness, the very same provision (Ethical Consideration 8–6) goes on to exhort lawyers to defend judges against unjust criticism. The code includes this solemn warning:

> While a lawyer as a citizen has a right to criticize such officials publicly, he should be certain of the merit of his complaint, use appropriate language, and avoid petty criticisms, for unrestrained and intemperate statements tend to lessen public confidence in our legal system.

As a result, it is no wonder that lawyers are reluctant to criticize judges or the way they perform their duties. Even when confronted with the most serious judicial misconduct, bar associations are usually loath to interfere.

THE CRIMINAL LAWYER

Only a small proportion of lawyers make a career of practicing criminal law, and most have no knowledge at all of how the criminal courts work or what their problems are. At one time the court assigned lawyers to represent defendants who could not pay a fee. Even that limited involvement has now been largely transferred to other auspices, first to those of the Legal Aid Society, and then, when private resources could no longer meet the need, to government-funded agencies, such as those sponsored by the United States Office of Economic Opportunity. For most attorneys today, criminal law is a strange and unknown world. They do not understand it, and they have no feel for its needs and problems. Entirely removed from its operations, they have no way of knowing whether or not it achieves justice.

Nowhere is the administration of justice more on display that in the processing of criminal cases. And nowhere is there more widespread belief among the general public that standards of morality have disappeared. People think of criminal lawyers as "mouthpieces" who will resort to any tactic to win acquittal for the guilty. Unfortunately, to some extent the public is right. It is not unusual for a defense lawyer to say that he would never represent an innocent man because he could not stand the responsibility. Given a guilty client, however, the lawyer is free to use any means at his disposal to try to get the man off. The emphasis on winning acquittals has changed the administration of criminal justice from a quest for truth and fairness to a game of fox and hounds.

Unfortunately this sporting theory of justice has crept into the legal profession's own framework of thinking as reflected, for example, in an advertisement for a recently published legal textbook entitled *How To Win Criminal Cases by Establishing a Reasonable Doubt*. The banner headline at the top of the advertisement read: "NOW . . . A VIRTUALLY INFALLIBLE MAS-

TER STRATEGY FOR BUILDING THE WINNING DEFENSE—IN ANY
KIND OF CASE!" The advertisement went on to describe many of
the high points of the book, with the implication that the
author ("a highly successful defense attorney") had used
these same tactics to win acquittals in "hundreds of cases, on
charges ranging from speeding to murder." Among the tricks
of the trade hawked to potential lawyer-purchasers were these:

> This new Guide shows hundreds of ways you can use the
> reasonable doubt strategy to weaken the prosecutor's case
> in just those areas *he must rely on to get a conviction.* For
> example:
>
> *Confessions*—How to defend against the confession, under-
> mine its credibility, actually *turn it against the prosecution.*
> Here is every move and counter-move spelled out—from
> pretrial confession hearing to winning summation tactics.
> Highlights the *best spot of all to attack a confession*—and
> just how to do it.
>
> *Evidence*—How to *identify and suppress damaging evidence*
> before the trial—how to use *grand jury testimony* to create
> doubt—how to nullify introduction of harmful evidence
> (weapons, drugs, photographs)—how to counter circum-
> stantial evidence and use it to lay your reasonable doubt
> foundation.

The adversary system is our method of trying to arrive at the
truth in judicial proceedings by presenting both sides of every
legal question and by challenging each assertion of fact through
cross-examination. But the attitude expounded here is the worst
sort of perversion of what this legal philosophy is all about.
To make a game of wits out of a serious proceeding in which
a man's liberty and the protection of society are at stake is a
grotesque charade. Just this sort of thing has made the general
public cynical about the administration of justice and the role
of lawyers. Unfortunately, these tricks to win criminal cases are
not limited to the occasional author of a sensational textbook.
They can be espoused by such highly respected legal organizations as the nonprofit Practising Law Institute, which recently

held a series of conferences on "Winning the Criminal Case Before Trial." The conference brochure announced that one major session would be concerned with "suppression of evidence, particularly evidence seized by law enforcement officers," and that another would cover techniques for suppressing the testimony of eyewitnesses. As the literature pragmatically noted, "Few offenders are caught on the spot; they are arrested someplace else at some other time. This means that any witnesses to the crime, whether victim or bystander, have to be called upon to identify the arrested person as the criminal." Lawyers were invited to find out just how to keep such eyewitnesses from testifying.

A common courtroom device used by trial lawyers is to divert attention from the facts of the case by attacking the adversary. The concept was articulated by Cicero: "When you have no basis for an argument, abuse the plaintiff." In modern times, the advice shared among lawyers is: "When you are weak on the facts, argue the law. When you are weak on the law, argue the facts. When you are weak on both the law and the facts, attack the prosecution." We can see this principle at work in the following transcript. (The transcript also discloses another favorite attorney's device—the asking of improper questions to get statements before the jury, even when you know that the court will sustain an objection to the question, although in this case, counsel actually did make an offer of proof to support the basis for his questioning and desisted when instructed by the court that he was circumscribed.) In this exchange, the defense lawyer conducted the following cross-examination of the FBI official called as a government witness:

Q. (*By defense counsel*) In recent times do you know whether the FBI has made it a practice to investigate various Black civil rights movements?

PROSECUTOR: Objection, your Honor.

THE COURT: I don't see any relevancy to this proceeding. Sustained.

Q. Do you know whether the Federal Bureau of Investigation investigated, prior to his death, the Reverend Martin Luther King?

PROSECUTOR: Objection, your Honor.

THE COURT: Sustained.

Q. Do you know whether, prior to her death, the FBI investigated and wiretapped Mrs. Eleanor Roosevelt?

PROSECUTOR: Your Honor, I object. None of these questions are relevant.

THE COURT: Sustained.

PROSECUTOR: I think they are improper and I think that Counsel should be directed not to pursue this line of questioning.

THE COURT: I will allow him some leeway, but they are perfectly irrelevant. I couldn't care less what they did with anybody back in what is almost the dark ages now. Go ahead.

Q. Have you heard that the FBI has been charged with having wiretapped the telephone of Hale Boggs?

PROSECUTOR: Objection, your Honor. This is completely immaterial.

THE COURT: The objection is sustained. That is just like the question: "When did you stop beating your wife?"

DEFENSE COUNSEL: When, your Honor, indeed.

THE COURT: Assuming as a fact that it did happen, which is absolutely improper as a matter of law.

Q. Do you know whether the FBI has investigated persons who have endeavored to send letters to Vietnamese POW's?

PROSECUTOR: Object.

THE COURT: Sustained.

Even though the judge sustained every objection to these highly improper questions, the defense lawyer succeeded in making his attack on the prosecution's witness. Since the jurors never heard the answers, they had to assume that what the lawyer was saying was true.

Our attitude toward the operation of criminal justice obviously needs overhauling. Justice is not a game. Prosecutions are not for sport. Laws are not enacted as the rules for tournaments. The American Bar Association recently sponsored an ambitious project to draft written standards of conduct for those involved in criminal justice. In one report the ABA committee went out of its way to criticize tactics utilized by some of the more noted criminal lawyers:

> In lurid autobiographical accounts, speeches and even at institutes, seminars and conventions of bar associations some of the more noisome lawyers have added to the confusion by speaking pridefully of their successes by use of tactics which at best were pettifoggery and at worst grounds for disbarment; they have recommended to their colleagues tactics and conduct which serve only to confuse the lawyer's concept of his function and to demean the entire legal profession.

The misfortune is that, aside from writing reports, the lawyers are not doing anything about it. Neither, at the moment, is anyone else. Chances are that nothing significant will be done until we develop a whole new approach to the job of policing the conduct of lawyers and setting standards of trust and responsibility that restore honor to a once-honored profession.

Chapter 3

The Judiciary—
Dependent and Independent

ON November 2, 1971, the voters of Queens County, New York, "elected" Seymour Thaler, a former State Senator, to the position of Justice of the Supreme Court of the State of New York. Actually, the voting was only a formality, since the political leaders had earlier reached an agreement under which Senator Thaler would be nominated by both the Republican and Democratic parties so that his election would be assured. Six weeks after Election Day, the Justice-elect was indicted by a Federal grand jury for dealing in $800,000 worth of stolen U. S. Treasury bills. Proof at trial showed that the judge had agreed to arrange for the redemption of the stolen bills and to divide the proceeds with three others in the scheme. Out of $250,000 in stolen bills which were successfully redeemed, the prospective Justice received over $93,000. The trial jury convicted all four defendants, and Justice-elect Thaler was sentenced to prison for one year.

In that same election, another judicial candidate received bipartisan nomination and was "elected" to the bench despite opposition from the bar association on the ground that he did not have the necessary "judicial temperament."

Over a period of five years, a total of eighty-eight out of ninety-seven judges "elected" to the New York State Supreme

Court received the nomination of both the Republican and Democratic parties in order to guarantee their election. In some cases these judges had already served one or more terms on the bench and were seeking reelection. But in many cases the arrangment was simply part of a deal between political leaders to divide up the available vacancies.

How is it possible that a constitutional system for the direct popular election of judges should be manipulated in this way to take control away from the voters and put it in the hands of the politicians? Why do we believe that popular election is the right way to pick judges anyway?

THE SELECTION PROCESS

One of the reforms demanded by the English knights who drafted the Magna Carta was that the king should select judicial officers only from those who were qualified and would obey the law themselves:

> We will not make any justiciaries, constables, sheriffs or bailiffs, but from those who understand the law of the realm and are well disposed to observe it.

Despite this royal commitment, the appointment of judges by the Crown, at least in the American colonies, left much to be desired. After adoption of the American Constitution following the Revolution, judges were chosen by popular election as a reaction against appointment abuses and as part of the movement toward judicial independence. Although perfect in theory, the concept of having judges approved by the people has turned out to be a travesty, particularly in large metropolitan areas. Where judges run with party labels they are usually swept along with the other candidates on the ticket, many voters never even knowing anything about the qualifications of those nominees they are thus voting in. In sophisticated urban voting districts, conscientious voters simply omit casting their ballot for the judicial candidates for this reason. Even where the voters are more knowledgeable about the candidates the chances

are overwhelmingly in favor of those nominated by the dominant political party.

Voter ignorance concerning judicial candidates is bad enough
in itself, but what it means in terms of the actual selection of
judges is a disaster. In many areas, the real choice is given over
to political leaders, who handpick their own candidates. All
the evils that once attended poor judicial selections by a des-
potic king are compounded by a selection process in which
political considerations are dominant. It is an open secret that
a judgeship is the prize sought by most lawyers in politics.
They spend their careers working loyally for a political organization in order to win that nomination for the bench. A young
lawyer may start out as a hardworking district captain and
stick at the job for years. In time he may become an assistant
district attorney, then a member of the state legislature. Perhaps
he may hold a position in municipal or county government.
Finally he receives the nod from his political leader. Twenty
years of undying political loyalty is not an unusual price to
pay for a judicial nomination. But what a price the public pays!
All along the way, whatever the position of public trust the
would-be judge may hold at the moment, when the political
leader asks for a favor he usually gets it. Most members of the
state legislature respond quickly to the crack of a whip from
their county political chairman. District attorneys with judicial
ambitions seldom investigate violations of the election laws,
improper political contributions or other misfeasances which
affect the electoral process. In many state legislatures, when the
leadership needs to enlist votes for a particular measure it is
customary first to summon the support of the local political
bosses, and to have them instruct their legislators in turn.
Probably the single most common incentive for this Yo-Yo
response to the wishes of local political leaders is the desire of
ambitious lawyer-politicians to receive the nomination which
they know will guarantee their "election" to the bench. Obviously not all elected judges follow this route, but far too many
do.

There is nothing inherently wrong with political experience

in the background of candidates for the bench—indeed it prob-ably provides a broad perspective and understanding of people —but the principal qualities of a good judge are intelligence, human decency, fairness and, above all, independence and in-tegrity. When the political process serves to destroy these latter qualities, then it becomes a negative rather than a positive force, and does harm to the whole system. The end result is poor judges—or worse.

Potentially the purely appointive system can also be abused, except that it tends to be out in the open where people can fix responsibility. While political leaders operate behind closed doors, mayors, governors and presidents must make their ap-pointments publicly, and must answer to the electorate if they commit serious blunders. Witness the public storm over Presi-dent Nixon's nominations first of Clement F. Haynsworth, and then of G. Harrold Carswell, to vacancies on the United States Supreme Court. Where the appointive system exists for state and local courts it has sometimes been improved by the estab-lishment of committees to screen nominees before they are ap-pointed, although this procedure can also be perverted. If the committee includes political allies of the appointing executive— it is possible to steer political cronies through the screening process with little opposition.

The appointment of judges works quite well for positions with high visibility, such as those in the Federal courts and the highest state courts. When it comes to lower courts, if little public attention is paid to the appointments less rigorous stan-dards can be applied with no one really getting excited about it. The principal way this can be offset is by adding a properly selected prescreening committee to review nominees *before* ap-pointment and provide for legislative public hearings *afterward* as a condition to confirmation. An essential ingredient is more active interest by the press in the quality of judges at this level. One special benefit from the appointive method is the frequent practice of conducting background investigations on the candi-dates. For example, all candidates for Federal judicial ap-pointments are carefully checked out by the FBI, which con-

ducts literally scores of interviews. No comparable procedure
exists for elected judges. But the real key to selecting good
judges is having the whole process take place in full public
view, and this particularly means that the bar, citizen groups
and the media must take a more active role in helping to expose
bad judicial appointments—hopefully before they are made.

ADMINISTERING JUSTICE

At the opening assembly of the American Bar Association
convention in St. Louis in August, 1970, Chief Justice Warren
E. Burger outlined a number of ills that have afflicted the court
system. He concluded: "In the supermarket age we are like a
merchant trying to operate a cracker barrel corner grocery store
with the methods and equipment of 1900."

The analogy is apt. State and local courts throughout the
country handle approximately 3,000,000 cases a year. The
Federal courts handle about 140,000. Ninety per cent of these
cases are processed in the lower courts, mostly in urban areas.
In thirty-two states there is no unified system of court administration, and responsibility and authority are scattered among
various state, county and municipal courts.

The most serious result of antiquated and inefficient administration of the courts is *delay*. Criminal cases take so long to
process that the courts actually become part of the breakdown
of law enforcement. Suspects either walk the streets without
restraint or rot in jails awaiting trial. Victims and witnesses
lose many days' pay and grow disheartened and cynical about
the judicial process. The crush of cases is so great that when
the time of disposition finally arrives, the courts and prosecutors are willing to settle for a plea of guilty to some lesser
offense just to clear the calendar. Meanwhile the question of
the defendant's guilt or innocence is compromised by a "deal."

Civil litigants also are hurt by delay, but their plight does
not receive as much public attention. Personal injury claims
usually wait many months and even years before they are

brought to trial. In 1971, delays of civil cases nationwide averaged 21.7 months. Delays of civil jury trials in accident claim cases can run as high as five years.

We have made some progress in reducing these delays. There is hope that they could be almost entirely eliminated if enough interest and resources were committed. The Federal and state courts in New York have adopted a rule for criminal cases requiring that the prosecution must be ready for trial within six months or the case will be dismissed. In the U. S. Attorney's Office for the Southern District of New York, the in-house rule is that most cases must be ready for trial within sixty days. Only the exceptional case may wait for the longer six-month deadline when trial preparation requires it.

One of the most remarkable techniques for eliminating delays was launched in February, 1970, in the Civil Court of the City of New York. Under the energetic leadership of Administrative Judge Edward Thompson, a new "Conference and Assignment System" was set up whereby judges work in teams of three. Each case is called before the Conference Judge (one of the three, who serves on a rotating basis) while the other two judges sit in adjoining trial parts. The Conference Judge calls up to fifty cases per day and attempts to settle, adjust or otherwise dispose of them. His success rate ranges between 60 and 70 per cent. The remaining cases are assigned to one of the two remaining judges for immediate trial. Cases are never returned to the calendar part; they are all processed through to final disposition. Lawyers originally resisted the new system, but when they realized the judges meant business by dismissing cases on default, they quickly responded. When the experiment began in early 1970, there were over one hundred thousand pending cases, some of them as old as ten years. Within two years that backlog had been entirely eliminated, and now the Civil Court of the City of New York is completely current. A plaintiff can expect to go to trial within a very few weeks of filing his complaint. This successful experiment shows what can be done if judges are tough-minded and apply themselves to the task.

Well-intentioned people—judges, bar associations, citizen groups, temporary commissions—have frequently addressed themselves to this problem of court management. While Band-Aid solutions have been developed and put into effect, the deeper problem of the courts' inability to cope with the work load persists. In January, 1972, New York City Police Commissioner Patrick Murphy, in a hardnosed talk to the Association of the Bar of the City of New York, lashed out in exasperation at the failure of the courts to perform their job. Commissioner Murphy said that the revolving door of the criminal courts had become a joke to most criminals. Not only do the courts fail to deter crime, he said, but every time a professional criminal walks away from an arrest unpunished there is increasing disrespect for the law. The Commissioner commented bitterly that every ten-year-old youngster in Harlem is said to know who the narcotics pushers are, while the police apparently do not seem to be doing anything about it. He said that the police arrest the pushers regularly but the court system routinely returns them to the street. Commissioner Murphy then leveled the bluntest charge of all. The court system, he said, was itself primarily responsible for the rise in crime:

> I will state emphatically that the court system must accept the giant share of the blame for the criminal rise in crime.
> We in the criminal justice system realize that the courts have problems, that money and time are needed, that the system wasn't designed to cope with modern violence and modern crime, nor with the criminal sub-culture in drugs. Some improvements to the system have been made already. Yet they have been too few and too slow. We can't wait much longer. Society can't wait much longer. Until the courts get more prosecutors, more judges, more courtrooms, the high volume of cases will interfere with the orderly movement of cases, maintaining this tremendous pressure to dispose of business. Clearing the docket will remain an end in itself and haste rather than intelligent and individualized deliberation will remain the result. Disposition by dismissal or by plea of guilty to a misdemeanor will remain the rule of the game with little attention given to anything else.

Law enforcement officials like Police Commissioner Murphy are not alone in their criticism of the courts' inability to administer justice. Many judges and attorneys agree. Why, then, is nothing done? Everyone seems to blame everyone else. Mr. Murphy told the lawyers at the City Bar Association that correcting the problem was their job. Judges say the fault is that of the Legislature for not giving them enough money and manpower. Lawyers come up with good suggestions for improvements, but nobody seems to listen to them.

The key to efficient administration of the courts is the development of good management techniques. Judges are simply not trained to run a mammoth organization that is in many ways similar to a major business corporation. As was pointed out in a staff report to the National Commission on the Causes and Prevention of Violence, judges have no professional training in how to organize or reorganize departments of the court, project program costs, establish manpower training and development programs, decide on computer processing, prepare space utilization and building programs, strengthen budget ties and working relationships with financial agencies outside the court, or build sound relationships with the legislature and executive. Yet these are all essential to the running of a modern court system.

Some steps have been taken to improve court administration in recent years, and several administrative offices have been established, charged primarily with the responsibility of compiling statistics. A real problem with these efforts, however, is that they seldom approach the situation from the perspective of efficiency. Moreover, the administrators tend to operate in the shadow of the judges who employ them, and therefore do not assert themselves against inefficiencies on the part of the judges themselves.

A typical example of wasted effort in the Federal court system is the existence in both the Administrative Office of the Courts and the U. S. Department of Justice of separate computer systems to keep track of pending criminal cases.

This is not only a complete duplication of resources, but it is also something worse, for the processing of the computers is so inadequate that both systems are fraught with errors and staff personnel must go through repeated crash programs to straighten out the inconsistencies that appear when computer print-outs from the two parallel systems do not agree with each other. Despite bleats of protest from some of those who must perform this thankless work, those who are responsible have such a vested interest in keeping the two systems running that there seems little prospect of eliminating the waste. Meanwhile, the manual record keeping which the computers were intended to replace must still be maintained.

A much more aggressive and intelligent use of management personnel and techniques is long overdue. Today's courts are big business and they should be run that way.

JUDICIAL MISCONDUCT

The emphasis on fair play in the courts goes back at least to biblical times. Witness this injunction from the Book of Deuteronomy:

> And I charged you judges at that time, saying Hear the causes between your brethren, and judge righteously between every man and his brother, and the stranger that is with him. Ye shall not respect persons in judgment; but ye shall hear the small as well as the great. . . .

Unfortunately, in many of our courts the small are not heard, and too often the great receive favored treatment. It is alarming how frequently special privilege appears to figure in the judicial system. In 1969, the nation was shocked to learn that the nominee for Chief Justice of the Supreme Court of the United States, then Associate Justice Abe Fortas, had agreed while he was a judge to receive twenty thousand dollars annually for services to a convicted stock manipulator while the man was under SEC investigation.

Many clients will select lawyers based on their belief that a particular lawyer has a wide acquaintance among judges and therefore will receive some special consideration when he appears in court. What a sad commentary on the judicial system—and, unfortunately, it has a certain amount of substance. Some lawyers do appear to receive special consideration from judges who are personal or political cronies. At least some judges certainly do not avoid the implication that such favoritism exists. Even today, it is accepted practice for law firms to send out engraved announcements like the following, when one of the partners becomes a judge:

(NAME OF LAW FIRM)

(NAME OF JUDGE)

HAVING BEEN APPOINTED BY THE
PRESIDENT OF THE UNITED STATES
A UNITED STATES DISTRICT JUDGE
FOR THE _____ DISTRICT
HAS WITHDRAWN FROM OUR FIRM

THE FIRM WILL CONTINUE UNDER
THE NAME OF (NEW LAW FIRM,
FOLLOWED BY LIST OF ATTORNEYS)

This form is perfectly acceptable according to present bar association standards. In the best light, it reflects a law firm's natural pride in having a partner appointed to high judicial office. But in another light, such announcement contains other implications for the lawyer or client who is looking for someone on the inside track.

One of the most graphic recent examples of political interference with the judicial process came during the 1970 trial of Martin Sweig, Administrative Assistant to former Speaker of the House John McCormack, charged with influence-peddling and perjury. A character witness called by the defense was Congressman Robert L. Leggett of California, who not only attested to Sweig's reputation for truth, honesty and veracity, but subsequently placed the defendant on his congressional payroll after the jury had found Sweig guilty of perjury. Congressman Leggett tried to soften some of the evidence of Sweig's

misuse of the Speaker's office by indicating that he followed
many of the same practices himself. During his cross-examination, he bragged that he often contacted judges on cases and
even interceded during grand jury investigations:

> Q. Will you tell us about those occasions, please, Mr.
> Leggett?
> A. Yes. I think one case was——I have different cases
> pending. As a practical matter none come to mind that I
> would want to talk about right now but you might get a
> request will you check into this. I will call a judge, I have
> very little trepidation about calling anybody, or call a United
> States Attorney. I will say tell me a little bit about what is
> going on. You know this guy is a pretty good guy, things
> like that. You got your job to do, the judge has his job to
> do. Judge, I don't want to intervene in anything being de-
> cided in front of the Court and certainly under the seculariza-
> tion of the bench from the lawyers, and I don't like to inter-
> vene in this, but many times you have people that have very
> important questions and they like to get as much insight as
> they possibly can, and certainly when we call a judge or a
> U. S. Attorney, we are trying to make sure they got the
> maximum background in a particular case.
> Q. How frequently do you call judges?
> A. It depends. I would probably say half a dozen times.
> Q. In connection with matters pending before them?
> A. Sometimes you don't know whether the matter is
> pending or not, you just call for information.
> Q. What kind of cases would you call judges on?
> A. It might be in a criminal case.

Apart from the possibility that they can be influenced by
friends or politicians, are judges actually corrupt? Do they take
money to affect their judgment in particular cases? Presumably not many do. But it is hard to know how extensive such
corruption may be, since proof is extremely difficult to come
by. Thirty years ago, the nation was stunned when a judge of
the United States Court of Appeals, Martin T. Manton, was
convicted for receiving eight different bribes in the form of
"loans" totaling $186,000 from parties in litigation before him.
In 1969, two justices resigned from the Supreme Court of

Illinois after a special commission of lawyers appointed by the court found that each of the jurists had acquired stock in a corporation whose principal stockholder was a party to litigation pending before the court. One justice had received the stock as a gift and the other at a bargain price.

In 1971, charges were filed against Justice Mitchell D. Schweitzer in New York alleging that he had engaged in a number of improper actions involving litigants in matters before him, including the release of an organized crime figure from prison after the convicted hoodlum had paid a fee to influence-peddler Nathan Voloshen. Justice Schweitzer resigned from the bench the day before the charges were scheduled to be tried.

On April 20, 1973, Judge Otto Kerner, of the United States Court of Appeals for the Seventh Circuit, was sentenced to three years in Federal prison after a jury found him guilty of bribery, perjury, conspiracy, mail fraud and income tax evasion. The charges related to a secret racetrack stock deal while Judge Kerner was Governor of Illinois, in return for which he assisted in obtaining favorable legislation and administrative rulings. Kerner and a fellow state official later realized a $300,000 profit on the stock.

Allegations of corruption among judges are frequent, but generally hard to substantiate. Many clients, however, are persuaded that it is entirely possible to "fix" a case. This attitude necessarily undermines any system of true justice according to which all men are supposed to stand on equal footing. Essential to the concept of justice is the guarantee of impartiality. Even one corrupt judge, or one fixed case, damages the cause of justice. As Francis Bacon wrote, "The place of justice is a hallowed place; and therefore not only the Bench, but the foot pace and precincts and purprise thereof ought to be preserved without scandal and corruption."

Various states have tried a number of measures to deal with judicial misconduct, none of them entirely satisfactory. The Federal Constitution provides for the removal of judges only for cause, and then only by impeachment. Many states also rely on impeachment, but because this is a cumbersome and time-consuming procedure, which requires action by the full legislature, some states have developed additional methods of removing or disciplining judges. According to one procedure, known as "Address," the legislature can on a two-thirds vote require a judge to resign or be removed by the governor. Another method, "Recall," requires that a judge submit himself to popular vote if a petition is filed charging him with misconduct; the judge forfeits his office if he does not receive a majority of the votes cast. Eleven states have "Courts on the Judiciary," composed of judges of the higher courts, which may consider a wide variety of charges against jurists, including misconduct or inability to perform functions. The sanctions include retirement, censure and removal. The most significant recent development in the disciplining of judges is the Judicial Qualifications Commission, first created in California. This commission is made up of judges, lawyers and laymen, and has the power to censure, suspend, retire or remove any judge found delinquent in his judicial activities. Approximately twenty states now have Judicial Qualifications commissions, and their universal adoption has been recommended by the Advisory Commission on Intergovernmental Relations. A recent study of judicial removal in New York compared the functioning of the New York Court on the Judiciary with the California Commission on Judicial Qualifications and concluded that the New York system is "cumbersome, inordinately time-consuming and inefficient." The Court on the Judiciary was created in 1947 at the urging of then Governor Thomas E. Dewey. Its purpose was to overcome the complexity and delay of impeachment by the legislature (a recent impeachment trial had taken two months of the Senate's time and cost $100,000, only to result in an acquittal). The New York court was convened only three times in the next twenty-three years, while California, a state of comparable size, during its first four years under the new Judicial Qualifications Commission received 344 complaints, conducted 118 investigations and brought about the retirement or resignation of 26 judges.

The real question, of course, is not how to remove corrupt

or incompetent judges, but how to keep them from getting on the bench. It is not enough to catch the wrongdoers. They must be prevented from ever putting on robes in the first place.

There seems little prospect of changing the method of selecting judges without an aroused public opinion. Bar association committees, legislators and civic leaders have on occasion urged reforms in the selection procedure, but their cries have largely gone unnoticed and unheeded. One reason is that in most states any constitutional change in the method of selecting judges requires approval by the state legislature, and since most legislators aspire to the bench under the existing system, they are not inclined to support a change which might deny them this prize.

At present it appears that the only way to arouse sufficient public interest in selection reform is by exposing so much judicial corruption and malfeasance that the public will demand that their legislators, always anxious to do something to please the electorate, take immediate action. The best form for any such change in the selection procedure is open to some debate. Judges still run for election in twenty-five states—on partisan ballots in fifteen; on non-partisan ballots in ten.

The first significant deviation from the election procedure was a "Merit Plan" adopted by Missouri in 1940, and now in effect in some seventeen states. This approach has been approved by the Advisory Commission on Intergovernmental Relations as part of its program of court reform. Under the Merit Plan, commissions consisting of representatives of the bench, the bar and the public screen and nominate candidates for appointment by the chief executive. Judges thus appointed are then required to submit themselves for a vote of approval at the end of each term. Efforts to extend the Merit Plan to more populous states have so far been unsuccessful. Probably the best method developed so far is nomination for appointment by the Executive, subject to confirmation after public hearings by the Legislative branch, as is done with Federal judges, together with some form of preappointment screening by a committee which includes lay members and sufficient public scrutiny through media coverage.

Make no mistake about it, the majority of the judges in this country are decent, hard-working, capable professionals, who conscientiously strive to do justice. But so long as there is any substantial segment of the judiciary that falls below these standards we cannot rest easy. No true, lasting improvement in the quality of justice can be achieved without improvement in the quality of judges and the levels of their performance. This calls for the following: an open method of selection based primarily on merit rather than political loyalty; disciplinary machinery to provide a continuing watch over judicial conduct and thus prevent any basis for a loss of public respect and confidence; and functionally sound administration of the court system so that cases move promptly, without waste motion or expense, to a fair and final disposition in which both the rights of the individual and the rights of society are protected.

Chapter 4

The Voiceless Poor:
Our Silenced Minority

ON January 15, 1973, two cases were called for sentencing
before a United States District Judge in Manhattan's Federal
Court. The first was *United States v. Velasquez.* A twenty-two-
year-old Puerto Rican woman with two children, five and four
years old, pleaded guilty to aiding in the theft of part of a
group of welfare checks amounting to a total of $2,086. The
woman had come to New York only a few years before, could
not speak English and was on welfare herself. She was living
with her husband in Brownsville, a poverty-stricken section of
Brooklyn. Her husband was a diabetic and she provided insulin
for him. She had no prior criminal record. The judgment of the
court: imprisonment for eighteen months.

The next case was *United States v. Delatorre.* An educated
white-collar defendant pleaded guilty to commercial bribery
and extortion in the amount of $23,000, as well as perjury and
subordination of perjury. The judge went out of his way to
point out, along with other considerations, that the defendant
had two young children and no prior criminal record. The judgment of the court: a suspended sentence.

It would be hard to find more graphic examples of the discrimination of our system of justice against the poor. All the
more dismaying is the fact that these cases took place in what

is regarded as one of the outstanding and progressive trial courts in the country.

Millions of Americans have studied photographs in newspapers and on television of the inmates of the nation's jails and prisons. Usually these pictures have appeared in connection with some protest uprising in an effort to improve prison conditions. How many Americans have remarked to themselves on the number of black faces in these photographs? Why is there such a high percentage of blacks in our prisons?

Certainly there is no support for a contention that blacks are more prone to commit crime than whites. That theory has been repeatedly exploded. In the military establishment, where blacks and whites are treated as equally as is possible, with integrated housing, training, eating, and working conditions, the offense rate is *lower* for blacks than it is for whites. Yet the fact remains that, while only 12 per cent of the nation's population is black, blacks make up over 40 per cent of the nation's prison population. Why is this so?

Most people cite environmental factors as the principal cause, and to a substantial extent they must be right. Poor housing, poor family life, poor education, lack of employment opportunity, inadequate health services, bad neighborhoods—all of these have an adverse effect on personality development. A study of youths in Harlem a few years ago disclosed that 50 per cent of the blacks under eighteen lived in a household in which there was no father. The impact of such factors was summarized effectively in a 1964 study by the American Jewish Committee, "Crime and Race":

> Thrust any child, white or colored, from the womb to a world that offers the rewards of status and success. With a moat of discrimination cut him off from the mainland so that there are few or no opportunities to achieve those rewards. Let him continue to wish for the same things the mainlanders desire, but make him move around much more, lose a father to death or desertion and a mother to work and dependence. Give him less knowledge to absorb, less money than the mainlander receives for the same tasks. Surround him with examples of unlawful achievers, and make him

fight to protect the mainland without fully participating in the rules to govern it. Shorten his length of life, expose him to disease, treat him as if he were biologically inferior and call him nasty names to convince him of it.

Yet we should still ask ourselves whether these environmental factors really tell the whole story. Do the adverse influences on poor urban blacks in this country explain why so many blacks end up in prison? One of the staff studies of the President's Commission on Law Enforcement and Administration of Justice (in the Task Force Report on The Courts) maintained that the higher incidence of crime and punishment among the poor is primarily a function of poverty:

> Poverty breeds crime. The poor are arrested more often, convicted more frequently, sentenced more harshly, rehabilitated less successfully than the rest of society. So long as the social conditions that produce poverty remain, no reforms in the criminal process will eliminate this imbalance.

Is that the complete answer? There are many indications that the system of justice itself discriminates against the poor, and that in at least three areas the poor do not stand on an equal footing with the well-to-do in the criminal courts.

The most shocking disparity between the treatment of the two groups shows up in the pattern of sentences imposed in criminal cases. It would be hard to prove that this was the result of any judge's conscious prejudice against the poor or against blacks, but the consequences are the same. The hard fact is that those who commit "common crimes," even though no violence may be involved, are the most likely to be prosecuted, convicted and sentenced severely.

In the Federal court system during the 1971 fiscal year, those arrested for common crimes received more and longer jail terms than those who committed white-collar crimes. Following are some examples of the difference:

71 per cent of those convicted of auto theft went to jail, for an average sentence of three years.

64 per cent of those convicted of transporting stolen property went to jail, for an average sentence of four years.

50 per cent of those convicted for stealing from the mails went to jail, with an average sentence of 2.6 years.

In contrast, those convicted of white-collar crimes, offenses that occur most frequently among the well-educated and well-to-do, ran a far smaller risk of being sentenced to jail, and, if sentenced, could count on a much shorter prison term.

35 per cent of those convicted of income tax evasion received jail terms, with an average sentence of 9.5 *months*.

22 per cent of those convicted for embezzlement went to jail, with an average sentence of 1.7 years.

16.3 per cent of those convicted of securities fraud went to jail, with an average sentence of less than one year.

The contrast between the treatment of rich and poor defendants is even more shocking in specific cases. In July, 1971, four defendants were convicted in Federal court for possessing stolen goods. The case involved approximately $5,000 worth of drugstore items, although the government's theory was that the stolen goods were part of a total shipment worth $63,000. One of the defendants was a laborer, thirty-four years old, married with two children. His family received $165 from public welfare every two weeks to meet their needs. The defendant had a record of previous larceny convictions. He received a prison sentence of three years.

A second defendant was forty-five years old, married with four children, living in an apartment in Queens that rented for $126 per month. His job as a dispatcher paid $125 a week. He received four years in prison.

A third defendant was an unmarried, forty-two-year-old unemployed laborer. He lived in an apartment for which he paid $125 per month. Psychiatric tests showed that he had a self-destructive personality and considered himself a failure because of parental rejection in childhood. He had undergone two business failures through no fault of his own. His record included several previous thefts. He received a prison sentence of five years.

It is to be noted that all these sentences related to a theft, involving no violence, of property whose maximum value under the prosecution's theory was $63,000.

In contrast, defendants from well-to-do circumstances convicted of sophisticated crimes received markedly different treatment in the very same court, even though the sums of money involved were substantially larger. In one stock-manipulation case, where the public was defrauded of four million dollars, the principal defendant received a one-year jail term and his co-defendants received terms ranging down to suspended sentences. The mastermind of the scheme was sixty-four years old, married with five children, and chairman of the board of directors of a national bank. He lived in an $85,000 home and earned $50,000 in salary each year, plus income from his investments.

In another case involving conspiracy to defraud the SEC, the trial consumed thirteen weeks, following earlier SEC proceedings lasting a year, and the principal defendant, who had made $500,000 from the scheme, received a two-year sentence. He was fifty-four years old, married and residing in a $150,000 home in the suburbs. His two codefendants, each of whom made over $150,000 through the scheme, received no prison sentences at all.

In yet another case, a lawyer who had formerly served as an assistant district attorney and then as commissioner in the city administration of New York, pleaded guilty to charges of failing to file income tax returns for two years, during which he had income totaling $147,000. His sentence was one day's probation and a $1,000 fine.

Another defendant was convicted of fourteen counts of unlawful trading on the New York Mercantile Exchange. The defendant, sixty-four years old, was married, had four children and lived in the Miami Beach area in a $125,000 home. He was a principal in five prominent Miami Beach hotels and also had an interest in two hotels in the Bahamas. In addition, he owned 30 per cent of a real estate corporation in New York City, and had formerly owned a major hotel in Las Vegas. His total net worth was over thirty-five million dollars. His punishment was a fine of $140,000—less than one-half of 1 per cent of his net worth. He received no jail sentence. While a fine of even $500 would be devastating to a poor man, a fine of this size was obviously insignificant to a man with such resources.

In those rare cases where blacks are convicted of white-collar crimes such as income tax fraud, the difference in treatment is marked. According to Federal Bureau of Prisons statistics, the average sentence handed down to whites for income tax evasion during the 1970 fiscal year was 12.8 months; for blacks convicted of the same offense it was 28.6 months—more than twice as much. During the same period, the overall average rate of sentences for whites in the Federal courts was 42.9 months, while for blacks it was 57.5 months—a difference of more than a year.

A second major area where our judicial system discriminates against the poor is in the availability of professional help. In recent years we have made a considerable effort to provide competent counsel for indigent defendants, and it is a tribute to our collective sense of fair play that we have made great strides. But we still have a long way to go. "Competent counsel" has not meant legal representation equal to that of the man of means, who can afford to utilize every procedural maneuver permitted in the court system in order to postpone or blunt the effectiveness of prosecution. Although many other factors undoubtedly come into play, the President's Commission on Law Enforcement and Administration of Justice noted that more defendants with assigned counsel plead guilty than those who have retained private counsel. The same is also true of those who are held in pretrial detention compared to those released on bail. Here is another area where a man's poverty directly affects the quality of justice he receives.

Many other aspects of professional assistance in the courts —the availability of experts, investigators, pretrial discovery and other services which may be important in preparing one's defense—differ widely according to the income of the defendant. And one other area of professional assistance where the distinction between rich and poor is especially sharp is access to medical experts. It is common for defendants accused of income tax fraud and similar white-collar violations to come up with opinions from psychiatrists and doctors attesting to their frail health and even temporary insanity. Many defendants who hire experts to give such opinions are able to avoid going to trial at all, or can at least minimize their punishment. There is no reason to believe that maladies and personality disorders are any less frequent among the urban poor—in fact the poor probably suffer from more extensive medical problems. But the indigent do not usually have access to medical experts who can help them avoid going to trial or to prison. Although there are some limited procedures for committing defendants to public hospitals for examination, these usually relate just to obvious mental disorders and insanity defenses. The more sophisticated medical excuses—such as weak hearts and "depression"—are available only to those who can afford to procure them. This discrimination in the courts is not right. If medical excuses are to be considered, they should be considered equally for all defendants. What is needed is some system that will provide the same doctors to rich and poor alike and apply the same yardstick of health and mental stability.

A third major factor accounting for the high number of poor blacks in the nation's prisons is the fact that persons jammed together in urban ghettos live out the most private aspects of their lives before the eyes of the police. People who live in squalor must use their stoops as a substitute for the living rooms found in the homes of the well-to-do. Consequently, their family squabbles and other disputes are likely to attract police attention, and frequently result in arrest. It is common for blacks to be arrested at some point during their adolescence, usually just "on suspicion." One highly regarded black legislator confided to the author that as a youth he had been arrested "on suspicion" while standing with three other teenagers on a Harlem stoop, and that the arrest record haunted him through his college and law school career and his efforts to be admitted to the bar. The experience is not unusual. What is unusual is that this young black overcame his arrest record and the bitterness that went with it.

The directive by a police officer to "move on" is a common part of life for the urban poor, and can also result in criminal proceedings, as is reflected in the following transcript of a case in the City Court in Syracuse, New York:

> COURT: What did you do? How did you wind up in jail here?
>
> DEFENDANT: I don't know. I was just standing there.
>
> COURT: I am going to give you ninety days in the Onondaga County Penitentiary but I am going to suspend that sentence on one condition, that in the future you don't give the cops a hard time. Am I getting through to you?
>
> DEFENDANT: Yes.
>
> COURT: One more time, and if you are brought in for anything like this again you are going up to the Penitentiary for ninety days. Do I make myself clear?
>
> DEFENDANT: Yes.
>
> COURT: The next time a cop tells you to move, you move, understand?
>
> DEFENDANT: Yes.

If a poor black does commit a crime, he is more likely to be turned in for prosecution than if he were white. Thefts of property are regularly reported to the police when they involve an intruder, but not when they involve an insider. It is common practice in business and financial institutions to cover up embezzlements by discharging the employee involved and requiring him to make restitution. Most businessmen, after all, do not want the embarrassment of having their customers or competitors know that there has been a dishonest employee in their ranks. When the criminal is a corporate executive, the chance of his being reported is smaller still. The business world tends to look upon the white-collar criminal almost with good-natured admiration, rather than with the contempt due a person who has betrayed his trust. While the violator from the ghetto will probably be arrested and prosecuted, the fellow who wears an old school tie may well escape with just temporary embarrassment.

These forms of injustice must be remedied. We should re-examine our entire enforcement policy as it affects the poor. Rehabilitative alternatives should be made available for those who have been denied the opportunity to develop good skills and positive personality traits because of unfavorable conditions at home. White-collar crimes should be prosecuted as vigorously as common crimes. Sentencing practices must be made scrupulously fair, without regard to the wealth or social status of the offender. Professional services should be available to all criminal defendants on equal footing. We may, indeed, have reached the point where all defense lawyers and medical experts should be paid out of public funds, so that the only difference a defendant's wealth would make is in the size of the fine or restitution ordered if he is convicted.

THE CIVIL SIDE

Although there has been much vocal concern about the plight of the poor in the criminal courts, we have generally disregarded injustices to the poor in the civil courts. Ironically, the civil courts—primarily in collection proceedings—have become paramount symbols of injustice for the poor. When the courts serve unscrupulous merchants and harsh collection agencies, they become instruments of oppression as threatening as the criminal court and the jailor. Economic imprisonment can affect one's freedom every bit as much as the criminal process.

There are three major sources of injustice in the civil courts: lack of legal assistance for the poor, court procedures which favor collection agencies, and a statutory bias in favor of creditors over debtors.

In affirming that the Fourteenth Amendment requires the provision of counsel for indigent defendants in state court criminal proceedings, the United States Supreme Court called for "fair trials before impartial tribunals in which every defendant stands equal before the law." Ironically, this objective has been limited to criminal cases. Why? Have we not reached the point when the poor have as much right to fairness in civil disputes as they have in criminal proceedings?

Put yourself in the position of a person of low income who has signed a sales agreement for a set of bedroom furniture to be paid for by installments. Then, assume that one of the following situations occurs:

(a) After the bedroom furniture has been delivered, you discover that it is not the same model that you saw displayed in the store and, furthermore, that it is defective. You make several telephone calls and personal visits to the store and receive promises that something will be done, but nothing happens. Finally, you refuse to make any more payments until the matter is straightened out.

(b) At the time you signed the installment sales contract you had a steady job and were able to make your payments regularly by careful budgeting. Then you became ill or were laid off the job because the employer was cutting back, and you were forced to miss several payments. When you purchased the furniture, the salesman assured you that if such a problem arose there would be no difficulty and that adjustments would be made in the payment schedule.

Now the court system comes into play. The furniture company wants payment and institutes a proceeding against you. Let us assume that you are actually served with a summons (although, as we shall discuss later, this frequently does not happen). You stare at the printed form which calls upon you "to make answer to the complaint." What should you do?

If you seek legal assistance, the chances are that you will not find it at a price you can afford. Neighborhood poverty law offices and legal aid societies are often understaffed or unwilling to take on the defense in a civil claim involving only a few hundred dollars. If you look for a private lawyer, where will you find him and how can you pay him?

If you should decide to represent yourself and deal with the attorney for the creditor directly, the chances are that he will want to have judgment entered against you before discussing a payment schedule. If you disregard the summons, either deliberately or because you do not understand it, then a judgment by default will be entered. Once the judgment is entered, a full range of collection procedures comes into play, the most common of which is the garnishment of wages. This means that a legal paper can be served on your employer and a regular amount deducted from your salary until the full amount of the indebtedness, plus added amounts for legal expenses, has been paid off.

Through all these alternatives runs one basic thread: you are never given a chance to defend yourself and have the dispute decided by a judge or jury. Where is the fair trial? Where is the impartial tribunal at which you stand "equal before the law"? A recent study of consumer credit by a team at Columbia University disclosed that out of more than one thousand persons against whom judgments were entered in collection proceedings, only seven ever had their cases heard by a judge.

Our concern, of course, should not be for the dishonest debtor who simply never intended to meet his obligations. But it is wrong to assume that all debtors are in this position. Indeed, as our economy has increasingly encouraged credit buying, more and more legitimate reasons are likely to arise for not making timely payment on installment credit sales. One recent study based on interviews with 1331 debtors in New York, Detroit, Philadelphia, and Chicago concluded that at least 20 per cent of those interviewed had valid defenses for withholding payment because of the creditor's failure to live up to his part of the original bargain. Interviews recently conducted by the U. S. Attorney's Office in the Southern District of New York have indicated that the incidence of valid defenses might run as high as 50 per cent in some groups. In other words, a substantial proportion of persons who default in making credit payments have an excuse that would be recognized in a court of law if those persons had a chance to defend themselves. When they are deprived of that opportunity, these people have every reason to feel bitter.

As it is, the civil courts are primarily devices for supporting the work of collection agencies. Frequently the collection agencies themselves engage in unconscionable practices which add to injustices against the poor. It is not unusual, for example, for such agencies to use dunning notices deliberately made to resemble legal papers. Sometimes they will employ actual legal summonses, even though a court proceeding has not been instituted. The effect of all of this is to add to the confusion for a debtor of limited education when he does receive a legitimate court paper. Another form of abuse involves the collection agencies' use of deceptive devices to determine financial data that might be used for collection purposes. In one recent case, a Harlem furniture dealer sent out forms emblazoned with an eagle and the legend "U. S. Funds Bureau." The form indicated that the headquarters were in Washington, D.C., and implied that funds would be disbursed if the recipient supplied certain data concerning employment and financial resources. In fact, the purpose of the form was just the reverse—to provide a basis for making a collection. Other improper collection practices utilized against the poor involve various threats. One company uses a form letter indicating that the customer's employer has been contacted and has advised that its policy is to dismiss any employee who has a garnishment filed against his salary. Such a policy would be illegal in most states, but since the creditor has not actually contacted the employer the entire communication is a double fraud. Collection agencies frequently make telephone calls to debtors claiming to be attorneys and threatening to have the debtors put in jail for failure to make payments. Such threats are particularly effective with the uneducated poor, who have no real knowledge of their rights.

The legislatures have consistently shown a strong partiality for creditors over debtors, and have enacted a series of statutes that operate to the disadvantage of the poor. This is not surprising, since substantial businesses and public utilities which are likely to be in the creditor class usually have lobbyists in the state capitals, while the individual poor are disorganized and without a voice.

The time has come to take positive steps to insure a fair hearing in American courts for all persons, regardless of wealth and station. Professor David Caplovitz, author of *The Poor Pay More*, has recommended several specific changes, such as establishing neighborhood consumer courts to insure easier access for the poor; outlawing door-to-door sales of expensive merchandise on credit (where the most unscrupulous practices usually occur); educating low-income debtors about consumer legal rights; and instituting a sliding-scale interest rate based on the credit standing of the purchaser. We also need a major overhauling of court procedures and remedies so that they apply equally to creditors and debtors (see Chapter 15). Above all, we must see to it that the poor are guaranteed professional legal assistance in the civil as well as in the criminal courts. Whether through a Public Defender concept, the allowance of attorney's fees to successful plaintiffs, or expansion of publicly funded Legal Aid, we must guarantee a fair trial before an impartial tribunal for all, rich and poor alike.

Chapter 5

Force and Violence

A FEMALE teller at a branch bank was recently the victim of an armed holdup. The robber escaped but was caught almost immediately and taken to court. A few days later, the teller was startled to see the same man standing in front of her cage. She panicked, dropped to the floor and pushed the alarm button, but the man did not budge. Cautiously she stood up and asked him what he wanted. "I'm out on bail," the man said, "and I need somebody to identify me so I can cash a check."

Despite its humorous note, this story tells a great deal about our system of criminal justice. Most citizens are completely bewildered by the way that system seems to defy common sense. Many criminals are never caught at all. Those who are arrested are usually back on the street in a matter of days or hours. Court proceedings drag on for months and even years. Many convicted criminals receive light sentences. Persons sent off to prison come back all the more hardened and professional, equipped to commit bigger and better crimes with even less risk of being caught. After all our expenditure of public funds and our endless commissions and reform proposals, somehow, somewhere, we have failed to control or reduce crime. Why?

Of the total number of serious crimes committed in the United States, only 50 per cent are reported to the police. A suspect is arrested in only 25 per cent of the crimes reported, and convicted in only 6 per cent of the crimes committed. Only 1½ per cent of all criminals are imprisoned. These are estimates of the National Commission on the Causes and Prevention of Violence, headed by Dr. Milton Eisenhower, based on an estimated annual total of nine million serious crimes, ranging from automobile theft to homicide. A Presidential Commission on Law Enforcement and Administration of Justice, under the direction of Nicholas deB. Katzenbach, earlier attempted to assess the scope of crime in the United States and recommend new techniques for coping with it. The Commission's final report, entitled "The Challenge of Crime in a Free Society," proposed several reforms in law enforcement and the administration of criminal justice, a number of which have since been adopted. But by and large, crime has *not* been reduced since the Commission's report was implemented. If anything, things have become worse.

Of greatest concern to Americans are crimes involving force and violence, the most frequent and serious of which are homicide, forcible rape, aggravated assault and robbery. These crimes make up approximately 13 per cent of the serious crimes classified by law enforcement agencies for statistical purposes and tabulated by the FBI each year in its published Uniform Crime Reports. The other serious offenses are crimes against property: burglary, automobile theft and larceny of amounts over fifty dollars. Interestingly enough, crimes of violence frequently are perpetrated on the victim by an acquaintance, or by a member of his family—70 per cent of homicides, approximately two-thirds of aggravated assaults and a high percentage of forcible rapes fall into this category. Robbery—the taking of property by means of force or threats—is the one violent crime most frequently committed by a stranger to the victim.

While suspects are arrested for only 20 per cent of the serious crimes committed in the United States each year, according to FBI statistics released in 1972, the resources of the police and the courts are drained by a huge number of arrests for lesser offenses. Some 21 per cent of *all* arrests in the United States are for drunkenness. The next highest arrest rate (9 per cent) is a tie between disorderly conduct and larceny, which are both followed closely by driving under the influence of alcohol (7.5 per cent). One obvious reason for our poor record in solving serious crimes is the diversion of law enforcement resources to minor offenses.

Many people have a mental image of criminals streaming from metropolitan slums into other parts of the community to commit crime. In actuality, most victims of crime are people who are concentrated in the urban ghettos. A recent study of the racial background of crime *victims* shows the following rates of victimization per 100,000 of population:

Offenses	White	Nonwhite
Forcible rapes	22	82
Robbery	58	204
Aggravated assault	186	347
Burglary	822	1,306
Larceny ($50 and over)	608	367
Motor vehicle theft	164	286
TOTALS	1,860	2,592

Similarly, a study of the income levels of crime victims shows those in the low income brackets to be much more frequently subjected to forcible rape, robbery, aggravated assault and burglary than those in higher income brackets. The reverse is true only when the victim's wealth is the criminal's particular target—when the crime is larceny of over fifty dollars, or automobile theft.

One would expect the largest cities to have uniformly high crime rates, but this is not necessarily so. The crime rate in Phoenix is more than twice as high as Pittsburgh, although only half its size. The crime rate in Denver is almost twice that of Chicago. Finding out the reasons for these differences may help us solve the larger problem. What, for example, is the effect on crime rates of better police work, employment opportunities, social services, schools and narcotics treatment programs?

Suburban areas are not immune to serious crimes, although it is still safer to live outside the city than in it. Crime rates in rural areas are only about one-quarter those of the central cities, while crime rates in the suburbs are about three-fifths as high as in the central cities. The rate of crime in the suburbs has doubled in the last decade. Between 1970 and 1971 the rate of crime showed increases of over 10 per cent in the suburban areas, rural areas and small cities, while in cities over a million, the increase was only 2.4 per cent. This change in the pattern has been explained in part by the increased mobility of urban criminals, combined with the much looser security standards in suburban homes. A sharp rise in drug abuse in the suburbs is also undoubtedly a contributing factor.

STREET CRIME

In many cities across the United States a substantial portion of the population simply will not venture out on the streets after dark. Women are particularly frightened, but many men share their concern. The reason is "street crime"—crimes of violence directed against individual victims. Of the crimes which cause the greatest apprehension, robberies (holdups and muggings) probably head the list, closely followed by burglary. Robberies present a direct concern for personal safety. Burglaries hold implicit threats for the householder who lives in dread of the time an intruder will appear at the bedroom window. There are almost 400,000 robberies each year, only 27 per cent of which are solved by the police. Burglaries number over two million per year, and only about 10 per cent of these are solved. Over half of the robberies take place on the street, and 60 per cent of all burglaries are residential. It is no wonder that people are deeply concerned about street crime.

The following is a diary of street crimes committed in a twenty-four-hour period in Washington, D.C., beginning at 8:00 A.M. on a Friday morning:

Friday, December 9:

9:15 A.M. Strong-arm robbery, street, $2.

10:00 A.M. Armed robbery, liquor store, $1,500.

11:30 A.M. Pocketbook snatched with force and violence, street, $3.

12:30 P.M. Holdup with revolver, roofing company, $2,100.

2:40 P.M. Holdup with gun, shoe store, $139.

3:20 P.M. Holdup with gun, apartment, $92.

4:55 P.M. Holdup with gun, bank, $8,716.

6:25 P.M. Mugging, street, $5.

6:50 P.M. Holdup with revolver, tourist home, $30.

7:00 P.M. Strong-arm robbery, street, $25.

7:05 P.M. Holdup with gun, auto in parking lot, $61.

7:10 P.M. Strong-arm robbery, apartment house, $3.

7:15 P.M. Holdup with revolver (employee shot twice), truck rental company, $200.

7:25 P.M. Mugging, street, $5.

7:50 P.M. Holdup with gun, transfer company, $1,400.

8:55 P.M. Holdup with shotgun, newspaper substation, $100.

10:10 P.M. Holdup with gun, hotel, $289.50.

10:15 P.M. Strong-arm robbery, street, $120.

10:30 P.M. Holdup with gun, street, $59.50.

10:53 P.M. Strong-arm robbery, street, $175.

11:05 P.M. Holdup, tavern, $40.

11:30 P.M. Strong-arm robbery, street, $3.

11:55 P.M. Strong-arm robbery, street, $51.

Saturday, December 10:

12:20 A.M. Strong-arm robbery, street, $19.

1:10 A.M. Strong-arm robbery, apartment house, $3.

3:25 A.M. Strong-arm robbery, street, $25.

3:50 A.M. Holdup with knife, street, $23.

3:55 A.M. Holdup with gun, street, $25.

4:20 A.M. Robbery with intent to rape, street, 75¢.

4:20 A.M. Holdup with gun, carry-out shop, $80.

6:25 A.M. Holdup-rape, street, $20.

6:25 A.M. Holdup with gun, tourist home, no amount listed.

6:45 A.M. Holdup street, $5.

7:30 A.M. Holdup with knife, cleaners, $300.

7:40 A.M. Strong-arm robbery, street, $80.

Robbery and burglary have been with us as long as man has been around. Literature is filled with tales of highwaymen, cut-throats, pirates and other bandits throughout history. The irony is that our familiarity with the problem has not helped us to find ways of dealing with it. One of the objectives of the National Commission on the Causes and Prevention of Violence was to analyze crimes of violence and develop new methods for dealing with them. Among the findings of the Eisenhower Commission were these:

The twenty-six American cities with populations of a half million or more contribute about 45 per cent of the total reported major violent crimes, although they contain only 17 per cent of the population. The six cities with populations of a million or more account for 30 per cent of violent crimes, although their population is only 10 per cent of the national total.

Street crimes are overwhelmingly committed by males, at a ratio of approximately 20 to 1. Young adults between the ages of 15 and 24 account for the bulk of robberies, assaults and rapes. Analyses of the employment background of individual violators show that over 90 per cent of those who commit robberies range downward from laborers to the unskilled unemployed.

Most serious street crimes are perpetrated by repeat violators. Those who commit robberies are very likely to do so again and again.

The United States has a substantially higher street-crime rate than other countries in the world. Our robbery rate is double that of Canada and nine times that of England.

The spread of drug addiction has had a dramatic impact on the incidence of street crime. Responsible law enforcement officials generally agree that approximately 50 per cent of urban street crimes are committed by addicts seeking funds to purchase heroin. In New York City the Commissioner of Correction recently estimated that 40,000 prisoners each year are locked up for crimes related to drug addiction, and that such addict-defendants make up between 60 and 70 per cent of the city's prison population.

Heroin dependency is a long-term affliction. Most addicts experience euphoria for a few weeks or a few months at most, then develop a desperate need for the drug just to keep them "straight." The problem is that this addiction is extremely expensive, often requiring the expenditure of between $40 and $100 each day, 7 days a week, 365 days a year. Not many lawful occupations can provide that much tax-free money above and beyond the other expenses of living, so most heroin addicts turn to robbery and burglary, or related offenses, to obtain the wherewithal to buy the drugs they need.

The FBI recently reported that the average burglary in the United States costs the victim $312. Since fences usually pay only twenty cents on the dollar, a typical burglary will produce only sixty dollars, about average for a hard-core addict's daily needs. This means that an addict who engages in burglaries to finance his heroin purchases must commit at least one burglary every day. It is no wonder, then, that the burglary and robbery rates have increased sharply.

FBI statistics sustain the theory that heroin addiction is largely responsible for the sharp increase in crime. During the 1960's, while the overall crime rate increased 148 per cent, the rate of increase for the crimes of homicide, assault and rape was well below the average, while those crimes commonly committed by addicts increased astronomically: robbery went up 177 per cent, larceny 198 per cent, daytime burglaries, 286 per cent. In analyzing these figures, the FBI commented on the very low rate of police success in solving such crimes: "This low clearance rate (less than one of every five cases) indicates the lack of deterrent and slight risk of detection." Burglaries are the most popular addict offense for just these reasons, with the result that a burglary is committed somewhere in the United States every thirteen seconds.

One of the most troublesome aspects of robbery is the use of weapons. A gun in his hand provides an unskilled, frustrated member of the community with a simple way to improve his economic power quickly, and turns a timid, insecure person into a menace to anyone within range. Unfortunately for potential robbery victims, obtaining a gun is simplicity itself.

Twenty-four million civilians in the United States owned handguns in 1968. The yearly increase in the number sold rose from 600,000 in 1962 to 2½ million in 1968. In 1971, 65 per cent of all homicides were committed with firearms, as were 25 per cent of all aggravated assaults and 41 per cent of all robberies. Handguns are the firearms most frequently used for criminal purposes. An analysis of cases where firearms were involved in a recent year showed that 92 per cent of the homicides, 87 per cent of the aggravated assaults and 96 per cent of the robberies involved the use of handguns.

In many parts of the United States, handguns are displayed in glass cases for sale to all comers. The only requirement of the purchaser is that he leave his name and address. Although after the assassinations of Martin Luther King, Jr., and Robert F. Kennedy—one with a rifle, the other with a handgun—a National Commission on the Causes and Prevention of Violence was established, we have not yet acted on the Commission's recommendation that we restrict the general availability of firearms. The predictable result occurred on May 15, 1972, when Governor George Wallace, campaigning for the Presidency, was shot five times outside a Maryland supermarket by a man armed with a handgun he had purchased openly in the Midwest. Only then did a congressional proposal to limit the sale of such weapons gain some momentum.

Is there anything we can do to cut down on street crime? The answer most decidedly is yes. The problem is that most of our efforts have been mere palliatives. Probably the most successful reduction of street crime so far has been achieved by the Metropolitan Police Department in Washington, D.C. In 1969, that city was known as the "crime capital" of the United States. Serious crimes had multiplied over the preceding years almost six times, and Washington ranked third among cities of comparable size in its rates for robberies, burglaries, murders and aggravated assaults. Reducing crime in the nation's capital became a special objective of the Nixon administration, and results after two years of the program were impressive. Between 1956 and 1969, serious crimes in Washington had climbed more than 500 per cent, according to a report by *U.S. News & World Report*, but between 1969 and 1971 they declined by almost 20 per cent. Among the factors given credit for this turnaround was an increase of 65 per cent in the size of the police force. Simultaneously, reorganization of the courts expedited the processing of criminal cases, more streetlights were installed in high-crime areas and new techniques improved relations between police and civilians.

But probably the most dramatic move was the establishment of a Narcotics Treatment Administration in 1970. Later in that year, Dr. Robert L. DuPont reported an 83 per cent drop in the arrest rate for former heroin addicts enrolled in the methadone program in Washington. Almost four thousand heroin addicts enrolled in the drug treatment program, and all concerned agree that reducing dependence on drugs sharply reduced addict crimes.

The Washington, D.C., experience underscores two points about street crimes. One is that we need vigorous police forces, backed up by courts which can move promptly and effectively. The second is that addict-defendants should be enrolled in treatment programs, not just run through the jailhouse and back out to the street, where they will commit more crimes.

We must place effective controls on dangerous weapons, especially handguns, if we are ever to control street crime. Such weapons continue to be available for purchase almost without restriction. While it is possible to justify the sale of some rifles and shotguns for hunting and sporting purposes, no reasonable argument can support the ready access to potential criminals of handguns, which have virtually no positive social values. Both the sale and possession of handguns should be absolutely prohibited except for use by law enforcement agencies. Controls should be enacted on the Federal level in order to insure uniform implementation.

How incongruous it is for our society to encourage the sale

and possession of weapons, and then for us to wring our hands when some unstable person uses a weapon to commit a crime. Yet we consistently react blindly and emotionally against any offender charged with using threats or violence, and we uniformly impose very substantial prison sentences in the vague hope that the criminal will somehow "learn a lesson." The problem is that such harsh punishment does not so much teach a lesson as teach the offender to hate society, vow that he will not be caught the next time, and return to the same pattern of crime just as soon as he is released.

Increasing the punishment for defendants charged with using force or violence has not improved anything, even though it may act to separate the violator from the outside world a little bit longer. If we are to assimilate these violators into society—and 95 per cent of convicted criminals are eventually released—we must reexamine our whole approach to crimes of violence and our techniques for dealing with the offenders.

We must stop using techniques based essentially on fear. A little thought would persuade us that many of those who commit robberies armed with a handgun are really not much different, as people, from those who commit larcenies using more sophisticated techniques. The difference is only one of method. The man with education and skills can use more sophisticated means for achieving his goal. The man whom society has not provided with such resources must resort to more rudimentary tools. It is primarily a matter of opportunity. The unemployed, uneducated black from an urban ghetto has a limited choice of means available. One of the most convenient that society offers him is the handgun or the switchblade knife. With these he is every man's equal, indeed master. Is there really such a difference between his personality and outlook and that of the educated criminal? Or is the difference one of skill, education and opportunity? We should pay more attention to overcoming these lacks rather than resorting to harsh punishment and repression.

Chapter 6

The Professional Criminal: Organized Crime and White-Collar Crime

ONE evening in a prison cell at Atlanta Penitentiary, the notorious organized crime leader Vito Genovese said to his cellmate, "You know, sometimes if I have a barrel of apples and one of those apples is touched—not all rotten, but a little touched—it has to be removed, for it will touch all the rest of the apples." When he had finished speaking, Genovese leaned forward and kissed Joseph Valachi on the cheek.

Valachi was petrified. He recognized the traditional "kiss of death" and understood that Genovese was saying Valachi had been condemned as an informer and was scheduled to die. Valachi immediately asked the prison guards to place him in solitary confinement. A few days later, as he was exercising in the prison yard he saw a man approaching him, and in his terror he jumped to the conclusion that this was Joseph DiPalermo, a fellow inmate Valachi believed had been assigned to kill him. Valachi picked up an iron pipe and blindly struck out at the man, hitting him across the head. He died. The man was not DiPalermo. Valachi received an additional sentence of life imprisonment for the mistaken homicide. By then he was so certain that he would soon be killed, under Genovese's sentence, that he sent a message to Federal agents saying he had something to tell them.

Joseph Valachi's was the most remarkable account of the structure of organized crime that has ever been made public. Appearing before a subcommittee headed by Senator McClellan, he gave detailed testimony about a vast criminal organization he called La Cosa Nostra. Afterwards many people tried to brush this testimony aside, but there was enough corroboration to persuade law enforcement officials that Valachi's information was essentially true.

Based on Valachi's testimony, the McClellan Committee issued a report in 1965 which concluded:

> There exists in the United States today a criminal organization that is directly descended from and is patterned upon the centuries-old Sicilian terrorist society, the Mafia. This organization, also known as Cosa Nostra, operates vast illegal enterprises that produce an annual income of many billions of dollars. The combine has so much power and influence that it may be described as a private government of organized crime.

The McClellan Committee report marked a turning point in both public and official attitudes toward organized crime. Long immobilized by factionalism, Federal law enforcement agencies began to marshall their efforts against this too-long-neglected threat. By 1967, the Katzenbach Commission was able to report on the extent of organized crime in the United States. The Commission disclosed that the core of organized crime consisted of twenty-four groups operating as "criminal cartels" in large cities across the country. Although allied with other ethnic groups, the members of these criminal organizations were almost all of Italian background,* with close bonds and a smooth-running system of discipline. The Commission reported that these organizations had thousands of employees performing street-level functions in gambling, loansharking and other illegal activities.

---

* It would be extremely unfair to brand Italian-Americans in general with the unlawful acts of the Cosa Nostra. In fact, it is probably more relevant to point out that some of the most creative, devoted and effective members of the law enforcement profession come from the very same background.

Historically, these crime rings had emerged after Prohibition and had gained their power through violence and murder. The most influential core groups were centered in New York, New Jersey, Illinois, Florida, Louisiana, Nevada, Michigan and Rhode Island. The Commission estimated that there were five thousand or more Mafia members in the United States.

According to the Katzenbach Commission's report, each of the twenty-four Cosa Nostra groups was known as a "family," with membership varying from as many as seven hundred to as few as twenty. Most cities were controlled by a single family, while New York City had five major families in operation. The Commission likened the organization of the Cosa Nostra to that of a large corporation structured in such a way that it could continue to function regardless of personnel changes. Even if a strong leader should die or go to jail, the business operation would continue. Except for the top ranks of "Boss" and "Underboss," the various positions in the organized crime hierarchy were given Italian titles, such as *Consigliere, Caporegime* and *Soldate* (also referred to as "button" men). Coordinating these families was a "Commission" that acted as the ultimate authority on organizational and jurisdictional disputes. This Commission, composed of the heads of the most powerful Mafia families, varied in size from nine to twelve men. At the time the report was written, the Commission was said to consist of five men from New York City plus one each from Philadelphia, Buffalo, Detroit and Chicago.

The secret of the success of the so-called Mafia has been the criminals' role in providing illegal services that large numbers of Americans want, or at least are willing to tolerate. Foremost among these is illegal gambling, which provides the principal flow of cash. Another significant source of profit is loansharking—the lending of money to people who do not qualify to borrow through ordinary commercial channels, and who are therefore willing to pay substantially higher interest rates, sometimes encouraged by threats and force. The Mafia also plays a major role in business and labor. Labor racketeering is particularly fruitful, since most businessmen are willing to pay a high price to achieve labor peace. Labor unions existing in name only have frequently been used for shakedowns of business firms. A sellout of the legitimate interests of working men is inevitable when established unions fall under Mafia domination. Mafia members have also been found in the operation of many legitimate businesses, including construction, food supplies, trucking, real estate, bars and restaurants, auto repair, dry cleaning, entertainment, vending machines, garment manufacturing and other lines of work. Monopolization, strong-arm tactics, extortion and, of course, tax evasion usually accompany the involvement of organized criminals in legitimate business operations. More and more, however, Mafia figures have been turning "respectable" and making safe legal investments of their profits from illegal enterprises.

Of all the activities in which organized crime is involved, none is more sinister than the importation, wholesale selling and distribution of heroin. Before World War II, the Mafia was behind almost all narcotics smuggling and distribution. Since World War II, with the institution of more stringent prison sentences, the increasing effectiveness of law enforcement and stiff competition from other organized groups, the Cosa Nostra has played a relatively smaller role in the narcotics trade, although it is still actively involved. New elements, from many different ethnic backgrounds, have taken over a large share of smuggling and distribution. The amount of heroin smuggling has increased so rapidly, however, that there are still huge profits to be made by all concerned.

The war against organized crime has produced some significant results in recent years. Most of the "bosses" named before the McClellan Committee are in prison or dead, although a new generation of leaders has grown up to take their place. Virtually all the recommendations of the Katzenbach Commission have been enacted and branches of a U. S. Department of Justice Strike Force against Organized Crime have been established in every major metropolitan area in the country. Although organized criminal activity has not been eliminated, there are signs that it is beginning to be brought under some degree of control.

That control can never be fully achieved, however, until two of the fundamental characteristics of organized crime are first effectively dealt with—corruption of enforcement officials and the silencing of witnesses.

Probably the most sinister aspect of organized crime is the corruption of government officials, and especially of those engaged in law enforcement. Sometimes entire departments are paid off by Mafia-controlled gambling operations. Such corruption occurs easily because the general public does not wholly approve of the laws prohibiting gambling. Virtually everyone feels that he should be free to gamble, whatever the statutes may say, and it is only natural that police officers assume there is little point in trying to enforce the gambling laws. The spread of legalized lotteries and off-track betting has contributed to this attitude, without significantly reducing the amount of illegal gambling. This is particularly true in jurisdictions where the criminal courts impose only token fines in gambling cases. Recently it has become apparent, however, that official corruption also extends to narcotics enforcement, and involves assistant district attorneys and possibly higher officials as well. Controlling such corruption obviously is of critical importance since the laws against illegal activities can never work while those whose job it is to enforce them look the other way. One useful step would be to give concurrent jurisdiction over local bribery violations to Federal law enforcement agencies. Corruption among municipal officials, permitting organized crime-controlled businesses to take over government contracts, is also increasingly common.

Another characteristic of organized crime which makes control so difficult is the code of silence binding virtually all who are involved in underworld dealings. For Mafia family members, this *omerta* is rooted in the instincts of loyalty and self-preservation. For those who transact business with Mafia figures, silence is based on fear. Many witnesses in prosecutions involving organized crime have disappeared, some without a trace. Unsolved murders are commonplace. Newspaper accounts of the gunning down of persons suspected of cooperating with the government make a very deep impression on potential witnesses when they are called upon to testify, frequently resulting in a sudden loss of memory or outright refusal to talk at all.

The prospect of a stiff prison sentence can sometimes make a defendant apprehended at the lower levels of illegal narcotics traffic agree to testify against his superiors in the hope of reducing his sentence. There is no such pressure to cooperate in gambling prosecutions, however, where the low-level operator usually expects only a nominal fine, or in corruption cases, which are treated like white-collar offenses and frequently draw sentences ranging from six months to a couple of years at most—much easier to face than the threat of harm at the hands of a Mafia muscleman. Until we use the leverage of more substantial prison sentences to compel lower-rung violators to testify against their bosses, there is little likelihood that we will ever put the principals of the Mafia out of operation for any extended period of time. Deterrence is about the only weapon society has for coping with the professional criminal. The prospects of rehabilitation are very slim. The one thing a professional criminal has to lose is a substantial portion of the years he has left to live, and the more of these years there are at stake, the more likely he is to think twice about continuing his criminal operations.

WHITE-COLLAR CRIME

Capital punishment was abolished in Russia in 1947. Over the ensuing years it has slowly been restored for selected offenses. Among the specific crimes which are now punishable by death in the Soviet Union are bribery, counterfeiting, speculation in foreign currency and embezzlement of public property. We call these kinds of violations "white-collar crimes" in America and punish them with little more than mild rebuke—seldom with even a prison sentence.

Although the forms of white-collar crime are as diverse and complex as skillful minds can make them, there are four broad categories. First and most obvious are the various forms of fraud and embezzlement, by which skillful white-collar criminals steal much larger sums of money than is available to the ordinary burglar. The most ambitious forms of fraud are in the securities field, where the biggest money is. One form involves the manipulation of the price of a worthless stock through artificial market activity—placing a series of false buy-and-sell orders to give the impression that the stock has suddenly become a good investment. It is possible to run a stock up from a value of zero to over forty dollars in a few days, and then reap huge profits by unloading a large block of it at the top dollar price. Another form of securities fraud involves trading in stock on the basis of inside information about business situations that would affect the price of a stock, sending it either up or down. Investors who take advantage of these anticipated price changes, of which others are unaware, can make substantial profits. It is against the law to speculate in stocks when more than a certain percentage of the money used is borrowed. One of the most popular ways to evade such laws is by means of secret Swiss bank accounts, through which an investor can place securities orders that cannot be traced.

Another common fraud in the investment field is the so-called Ponzi scheme, whereby investors are promised huge profits which turn out to be paid from their own original cash investment. The first victims enrolled in such a scheme are so gleeful at the big returns they are apparently receiving that they unwittingly bring other victims into the scheme, until there are enough to make it worthwhile for the promoter to run off with the dollars that have been put into his hands.

Embezzlements from banks, brokerage houses and other business institutions constitute a major portion of white-collar crime. Essentially these embezzlements are simple thefts, on the same plane as a robbery or burglary, but they usually involve more elaborate methods of concealment.

A second broad category of white-collar crime includes bribes and kickbacks. In a common form of labor racketeering, management will avoid costly strikes by making under-the-table payments to labor officials who are willing to sell out the rank-

and-file union members. Corporate executives argue that these illegal payments protect the rights of their stockholders, but they cost dearly in kickbacks and extortion over the years. Kickbacks are also common on government procurement contracts and other dealings involving government agencies. Bribery is often inspired by the businessman's desire to get government approval for some action, or to fix a proceeding over which a government official has control. Bribes can run anywhere from the ten dollars to avoid a speeding ticket to the hundred thousand dollars to buy off a securities-fraud investigation. Commercial bribery involves secret payments in order to get or hold lucrative contracts.

A third significant category of white-collar crime is income tax evasion. As income tax levels have risen sharply in recent years, so have the incentives to cheat on tax returns. An unscrupulous taxpayer who pads expenses with false invoices or diverts income to dummy recipients can literally steal many thousands of dollars from the public coffers. Despite the resentment we all feel when we are filling out our own tax returns, we have no reason to sympathize with the taxpayer who deliberately commits fraud to conceal his true tax liability and thereby makes the rest of us pay more than our fair share.

The fourth broad category of white-collar crime includes the various specific business violations, such as deliberate transgressions of the antitrust laws through price-fixing and collusive bidding. The courts have begun to pay serious attention to business crimes which prey on consumers. Recently there have been many more prosecutions against those who use fraudulent selling or collection practices.

During the nineteenth century the American public tended to wink at a businessman's overreaching because business was enjoying a period of explosive economic growth from which everyone seemed to benefit. As the economy has matured, we have come to understand that each white-collar violation has a significance far greater than the amount of money that may be involved. Because those who engage in white-collar crimes tend to attract public attention when they are arrested and prosecuted, their misconduct is paraded before the rest of the world. When the poor man sees the white-collar criminal able to obtain the aid of experienced lawyers who can prolong the proceedings, take advantage of every technicality and obtain favored treatment from the courts, then the impact of white-collar crime is compounded, for here is direct evidence of injustice in the way the courts are run.

A major cause of white-collar crime is the attitude of business and professional men. Just as one of the most important factors behind drug abuse is peer influence, the attitudes of a man's colleagues contribute to the commission of white-collar crimes. As long as businessmen wink at their associates' unethical and illegal practices—or even worse, smile in apparent approval—white-collar crime will be with us. Although law enforcement offices can continue to prosecute the occasional violator and hope to hold up his example as a deterrent to others, we will make no real progress in curbing white-collar crime until businessmen themselves decide to do something about it. That means setting a good example at the top; speaking up against improper actions by others; discouraging commercial bribery and gifts to public employees; straightening out any suggestion of impropriety immediately; consulting a lawyer regularly for guidance; keeping alert for extravagance; and promptly reporting all irregularities to the authorities.

Although businessmen have a major share of the responsibility for curbing white-collar crime, the job does not end with them. What also is needed are adequate investigative resources, a firm commitment by those in law enforcement to give high priority to white-collar prosecutions and the establishment of a single standard of justice for all defendants who are convicted of crime in our courts.

From the standpoint of the administration of justice, the organized crime figure and the white-collar criminal have much in common. Both are deliberate violators of the law who are motivated by illegal profits. Both prey on the vices and avarice of other human beings. Both are favored in the courts and can take advantage of every legal procedure and loophole with help from high-priced counsel and, too often, a friendly attitude from the bench.

Public attitudes play a large part in the nurturing of organized and white-collar crime. A tolerant view toward illegal gambling, corrupt practices and cheating on taxes provides fertile ground for the well-manicured operator to move in and reap huge illegal gains. Obviously part of the job of reining in these professional criminals falls to the "decent" elements of the community who must take a more affirmative approach to creating an atmosphere of disapproval toward such conduct. But we know enough about human character to recognize that both organized and white-collar crime will still continue on a substantial scale unless there is also a much more positive law enforcement effort to keep it within minimum bounds.

The starting point for more effective law enforcement action against organized and white-collar crime is better resources and direction. By and large this responsibility is a Federal one, since most of these illegal activities extend far beyond the jurisdictional limits and capabilities of local law enforcement agencies. To be sure, many outlets for organized crime such as gambling, narcotics sales, loan sharks, and businesses and labor unions which have come under Mafia domination, operate on the local level. That explains the pressure for corrupting local officials to buy "protection." But the real nerve center of these operations, where any lasting impact must be felt, usually involves multistate relationships and requires well-organized intelligence gathering and extensive investigative manpower of the type that is seldom available to a local agency. Hence the recent establishment of Joint Strike Forces against Organized Crime under the U. S. Department of Justice in every major metropolitan center in the country.

The Federal Strike Forces theoretically bring together the resources of virtually all Federal enforcement agencies into a team operation. The reason for setting up the Strike Force structure in the first place was the failure of Federal law enforcement agencies to cooperate with each other in any meaningful way. A tradition of bureaucratic provincialism existed which made Federal law enforcement virtually muscle-bound when it came to sharing information about criminal conduct and developing a coordinated enforcement attack so that every violation of law might be considered for possible prosecution.

The Federal Strike Forces have now been in operation for about five years, and although much progress has been made in breaking down barriers between agencies, the program still leaves much to be desired. National leadership of the Strike Force program is thin, generally unimaginative and doctrinaire. After five years, investigative resources are still directed primarily against local gambling operations instead of the more sophisticated invasions of legitimate business and international operations by organized crime. The FBI, although it uses all the right words about cooperation with other agencies, has held back on its support of the program and has been leaden-footed in investigating corruption among local law enforcement offices—the *sine qua non* of much organized crime activity—apparently on the premise that the agency would rather maintain friendly relations with local police departments than take on the unpleasant job of eliminating practices which destroy their effectiveness.

The law enforcement resources available for dealing with white-collar crime on the Federal level are no better. As noted in Chapter 8, the investigative staff of the SEC is woefully inadequate. The IRS investigative staff is also far below minimum levels, which is particularly ironic since dollar-for-dollar there is no area where Federal appropriations can show such a large financial return. IRS agents produce ten to twenty times their annual salary in additional tax assessments. Beyond these two agencies is a huge void in Federal investigative resources to fight white-collar crime. There is no agency, for example, with primary jurisdiction over misuse of secret foreign bank accounts or criminal consumer fraud practices. The Postal Inspection Service will sometimes pitch in with manpower if requested, and occasionally one can persuade the FBI to take a specific case, but no Federal agency is keeping a steady lookout for white-collar crime across the board. This leaves the job to the ingenuity of the local United States Attorney, who is supposed to be a prosecutor rather than an investigator, and puts the burden on him to find the necessary manpower and to give direction to any investigative effort. Recently a tiny handful of investigators have been assigned to a few major U. S. Attorney's offices to help fill the gap, but there is still a long way to go. The real fault lies with congressional neglect of the problem.

Apart from investigative resources and coordination, the other main tool for effective legal control of organized and white-collar crime rests with the courts. Lawyers retained by these violators are the best that money can buy, and they usually run rampant through the full range of procedural remedies originally designed to assure due process for the downtrodden. Criminal proceedings can drag on for years, while witnesses lose heart or nerve, and the increasing possibility of some procedural error improves the chances for the defendant to escape ultimate justice. The attitude of judges toward these offenders is sometimes appalling. We have noted elsewhere the contrast in sentencing between white-collar and common criminals. Privileged treatment for organized crime defendants has also been observed. A recent legislative inquiry in New York State disclosed a substantial number of cases where Mafia figures received nominal sentences and other favored treatment from judges. Here the magic ingredient often is the politically placed attorney who appears before the politically oriented judge. Time and again special deference is paid to the political lawyer who represents an organized crime defendant before a judge who owes his robes and his hoped-for reelection to a political leader. The remedy for this, of course, is better methods of selection for judges, and public exposure of every miscarriage of justice that benefits the favored few.

Chapter 7

Overcrowding and Delay in the Criminal Courts

ONE of the most successful criminal defense lawyers in the country, Edward Bennett Williams, recently caused a stir when he lashed out at the inability of our criminal courts to deter crime:

> The criminal courts of troubled urban America are failing wretchedly. Like scarecrows put in the fields to frighten the birds of lawlessness, tattered and unmasked from neglect, frightening to no one, they have become roosting places for the crows. To the innocent, to the victims of crime, to the witnesses to crime, to the illiterate, the uneducated, and the poor, many of our big city criminal courts are a sham and a broken promise.

Law enforcement officials have also become increasingly outspoken in their criticism of the court system and its failure to deal with the criminals who are arrested and brought to justice. The following comments were made by Patrick V. Murphy, who was then New York City's Police Commissioner:

> We, the police, are far from perfect, but we have shouldered the entire blame long enough. We, the police, are more efficient today than ever. We pour arrested criminals into the wide end of the criminal-justice funnel, and they choke it up until they spill over the top. And when I say spill over—they spill over the street and commit more crime.

So we arrest them again, pour them into the funnel as far as the court system again, and they spill out again. And the cycle repeats itself day after day after day. . . .

Commissioner Murphy said that the New York City Police Department had increased the number of felony arrests between 1960 and 1970 from 35,629 to 94,042, a rise of 165 per cent. Only 552 of these cases actually went to trial, the rest being disposed of primarily through plea bargaining and dismissals. This result, he said, was discouraging for the dedicated policeman, who has come to feel that conscientious police work is a waste of time. The Commissioner complained that the court system was not dealing with the criminals arrested by the police, and instead was turning them out on the street to wait for months and even years before their cases came to trial, while during the interval they continued to commit more and more crimes.

SLOW-MOTION JUSTICE

Delay in the prosecution of criminal cases is undoubtedly our most serious law enforcement problem today. For the defendant, delay usually means months and even years of uncertainty, while charges hang unresolved over his head. For society, delay means that wrongdoers are not brought to justice promptly enough and that the correction process is not put into operation when it counts. For law enforcement agencies, delay means loss of evidence and loss of drive.

The best way to deter crime is to assure potential criminals that they face arrest, prompt prosecution and commensurate punishment. When criminals no longer fear effective law enforcement, crime rates go up and criminals find more victims.

One of the causes of delay is a general lack of initiative and momentum in the courts. By and large, judges are content to wait until the litigants are ready to go to trial. There is too little emphasis on effective administration of the courts by the trial judges themselves. A number of judges are doing an excellent job of bringing their calendars under control, but many others still follow a lazy laissez-faire policy.

Defense counsel are also a major source of delay. Although defendants' lawyers frequently claim "prejudice" to their clients from delay in criminal cases, they are all too frequently the principal causes of that delay, repeatedly seeking adjournments and postponements of the day of trial. Sometimes defense counsel seek adjournment in hopes that delay will benefit their clients as testimony and other evidence fall by the wayside with the passage of time. Usually, though, the defense bar is over-worked and cannot cover all of the courts at once. It is essential that we provide enough qualified private and publicly supported defense lawyers to do the job.

One of the principal causes of delay in the courts is the crushing volume of cases. The number of criminal prosecutions continues to jump each year, and not simply because there is a rise in crime; the increase is also due to the fact that the state legislatures and Congress enact additional criminal sanctions at virtually every session. The pat remedy for any social ill that cannot be otherwise cured is to make those involved chargeable with a crime. The Federal courts alone have enormously expanded criminal jurisdiction in such areas as civil rights violations, environmental damage and consumer fraud in the past few years. Of course some of these matters belong in the criminal courts, but many do not.

There is increasing waste motion in the criminal courts, as evidenced by the growing frequency of dismissals and acquittals. Between 1959 and 1969 the number of misdemeanor cases in the courts of New York State increased slightly more than 10 per cent, while the number of dismissals and acquittals rose almost 100 per cent, from 88,607 in 1959 to 165,927 in 1969. In the meantime the number of successful convictions actually *decreased*. That dismissal figure represents an almost complete waste of law enforcement effort.

How can we possibly justify the cost in time and money which the huge volume of cases that result in dismissals involves for police officers, court personnel, witnesses, jurors, judges, prosecutors, and defense counsel? How can we justify the cost even in cases which result in suspended sentences or minimal fines? Why do we utilize judicial machinery at all to cope with personality disorders, narcotics addiction and other illnesses? If we are to get at basic causes of delay, we must remove much of the extraneous business that currently clutters the criminal courts and save that machinery for cases involving human liberty, where it really can be used effectively.

A number of courts and state legislatures have recently adopted rules requiring the trial of criminal cases within a specified period of time, under threat of dismissal. The problem with such speedy-trial rules is that they are not enforceable as far as the judge is concerned. While the prosecutor may be ready for trial, the judge may be slow in scheduling his cases, so that the system begins to slow down all over again. On the other side of the coin, some judges will not listen to legitimate reasons for postponing a case. In one recent Federal case of a lawyer charged with arranging for perjured testimony in a narcotics trial, the District Court judge dismissed the indictment when the government's principal witness disappeared, thus permitting the defendant to walk out as a free man. When a case is dismissed, society pays the price. Another aspect of the problem that has still not been adequately dealt with is the long period of time consumed in appeals from convictions. Very often defendants remain free on bail while their appeals slowly wend their way through the appellate process, frequently much more drawn out than the original trial itself. Even though a defendant has been adjudged *guilty* by a trial jury, he is permitted to roam the streets unfettered while the appellate process grinds along at its leisurely pace.

VICTIMLESS CRIMES

Victimless crime is so overwhelmingly pervasive throughout the country that dealing with it through criminal penalties misuses our policeman power, congests and makes a travesty of our courts, and jams the jails. It so preoccupies the criminal justice system that it prevents it from dealing effectively with real crime.

These angry words were issued by the National Council on Crime and Delinquency, headed by Carl M. Loeb, Jr., in a booklet urging basic revisions of the criminal laws. Victimless crimes are also called "consensual crimes"—those offenses, such as drunkenness, gambling, drug use, prostitution and vagrancy, in which usually the only person hurt is the one who is engaged in the activity. There is no victim as there is in a robbery or rape.

The statistics concerning victimless crimes are sobering: it is generally accepted that *half* of all arrests made by policemen through the nation are for victimless crimes, and that *half* of all people in jail are being held in connection with such crimes. If all this business were removed from the courts, it is argued, then the problems of congestion and misuse of police and judicial manpower would be dramatically affected. There is much force to this argument, but the arithmetic is not quite as simple as it seems. Although half of the cases taken to court may involve victimless crimes, these cases do not take up half of the court time, since they are usually handled on a wholesale basis. A single judge will process literally hundreds of these prosecutions each day, where a serious violation may take up several days or even weeks or months of court time. Nor are all these offenses without criminal significance. Large-scale gambling is usually associated with organized crime and produces revenue which is then put to use in loansharking, narcotics traffic and similar illegal activities. Organized prostitution may also take on this character. Nonetheless, we have good reason to take a new look at victimless crimes.

It is self-evident that the use of drugs has not been significantly halted by the existence of criminal sanctions against possession. But that does not mean that we should rush into full legalization of drugs. Not many people seriously propose a no-holds-barred legalization of heroin, although many have advocated such an approach with respect to marijuana. Until we are certain that unrestricted use of marijuana is truly harm-

less and will not in any substantial number of instances lead to
heroin addiction, no real case can be made for its outright
legalization. On the other hand, almost everyone seems to agree
that the sanctions must be reduced. Use of marijuana should
not be classed as a felony but as an offense or misdemeanor. A
good parallel would be our restriction of the sale of fireworks,
purely for the purpose of discouraging their widespread use
and the possibility of physical harm. Such an approach should
be applied to the personal use of drugs, combined with provision for treatment of the addict offender. Society should take
advantage of every opportunity to turn the addict away from
his dependency, and the attendant need to commit crimes in
order to finance it.

Our concept of vagrancy is Puritan in its origins. The notion
that it is a crime to loiter simply makes no sense at all. The
obvious substitute for prosecution must be social services to
care for the derelict in a humane fashion.

Our laws regarding prostitution and other criminal violations
based on sex are certainly out of phase with an age which has
virtually abandoned any attempt to control the impact of porno-
graphic materials. Prostitution should be regarded primarily as
the public health problem it actually is, requiring some form of
licensing and inspection to protect customers against the spread
of disease. There is no reason to perpetuate the practice of
arrests, shakedowns and corruption which largely characterize
criminal enforcement in this area.

Of all the victimless crimes which commend themselves to
a new approach, drunkenness stands out as one most in need
of change. According to the National Council on Crime and
Delinquency, one-third of all arrests in the United States are
for some form of drunkenness. Yet our impact on the problem
of alcoholism has been nil. A study in Washington, D.C., a few
years ago, dramatized the futility of criminal prosecutions for
alcoholics. Researchers turned up *six* defendants who had col-
lectively served 125 years in penal institutions and who had
been arrested a total of 1,409 times for drunkenness in their
lifetimes. It was estimated that the cost of arrests and prosecu-

tions for these six men alone amounted to some $600,000, and yet never once did a court deal directly with the causes of the basic problem—alcoholism.

The U. S. Public Health Service and the National Institute of Alcohol Abuse and Alcoholism contend that any person with a drinking problem can be helped as long as rehabilitation resources are available and the problem is met with acceptance and understanding. Those agencies also point out that skid row derelicts comprise only about 5 per cent of the total number of alcoholics, and that fully half of the alcoholics in the country are employed in full-time jobs. How unjust it is to apply criminal sanctions against those unfortunates who happen to be at the flophouse end of the alcoholic spectrum.

Some cities have recently begun experimenting with different approaches to drunkenness. In Philadelphia, where 43 per cent of all arrests are for drunkenness, a defendant in such a case can now be released without a court hearing if a relative calls for him. In New York City, the Vera Institute of Justice, in a cooperative program with the New York City Police Department, has conducted patrols on the Bowery and other known haunts of alcoholics to persuade drunks to go voluntarily to a special infirmary for treatment. Seventy-five per cent of those approached by the special patrol responded immediately, and many others did later. This kind of program certainly makes more sense than burdening the criminal courts.

The most perplexing of the victimless crimes is gambling. Increasingly, public opinion seems to favor the legalization of gambling both as a source of public revenue and as a way of eliminating the problem of gambling enforcement, with all its risks of official corruption. The basic problem with this approach is that gambling is not a simple indulgence. For too many people, gambling is a compulsion almost as serious as drug addiction and alcoholism. A gambling habit often leads to the commission of crimes to obtain funds for paying off gambling debts. Legalized gambling has provided the incentive for public officials accepting bribes to finance visits to the race track, and bank employees stealing to finance trips to the gambling casinos.

Seeking a solution to the gambling problem is complicated, but that does not mean we should not try. The important thing is to halt the charade of gambling enforcement we are tolerating now. Nothing can more graphically portray the inadequacy of our present criminal law approach than a recent report issued by the New York State Commission of Investigation, under the effective chairmanship of Paul J. Curran. The SIC report referred to an anonymous letter its chairman had received in 1967 identifying the "Imperial Social Club" at 646 Morris Avenue in the Bronx as a center of illegal gambling activities. The State Commission turned the letter over to the New York City Police Department for appropriate action. A year later, the Police Commissioner indicated to the SIC that after an investigation of gambling activities at the club and in the surrounding area, police had made approximately twenty gambling arrests.

Nonetheless, the Commission received a second letter in June, 1970, and a third letter in February, 1971, maintaining that gambling activities were continuing unchecked at the Imperial Social Club. Again the SIC turned the allegations over to the appropriate enforcement officials, and in March of 1971 it received a comprehensive report from the office of the Bronx District Attorney, which indicated that the Police Department had made eighty-eight gambling arrests between February, 1970, and January, 1971, in the vicinity of the Imperial Social Club.

The SIC decided to investigate each of the arrests. The results were dismaying. Approximately 40 per cent had resulted in dismissals before trial or acquittals because of defects in police procedures. Forty-seven of the arrests resulted in convictions, with pleas of guilty being entered in virtually every one of the cases. Each of the forty-seven defendants received fines, ranging from $25 to $250, totaling $3,750. Only one defendant in the entire group went to jail, and he served a five-day sentence by choice rather than pay a $50 fine. Aside from the amount of courtroom time that was expended on these cases, police manpower was utilized for surveillance of the suspected area on 102 separate days. The cost of all this enforcement effort obviously far exceeded the amount of the fines that were imposed.

Of much greater significance, however, was the absence of any deterrent effect after all this police work. The criminal records of some of the defendants are revealing: one defendant, who was fined fifty dollars on a plea of guilty to possessing gambling records, had five separate aliases and a criminal record extending back to 1933, when he had been convicted of counterfeiting. He had been arrested on forty-six previous occasions, twenty-four times for gambling, and had been convicted on fourteen of the prior arrests, seven times for gambling offenses. His most recent gambling conviction had occurred less than one month before the conviction for activities at the Imperial Social Club. One of his other convictions had resulted in a twelve-year prison sentence for sale of counterfeit money. Against this background, the process of arrest, conviction and imposition of a fifty-dollar fine must have seemed humorous indeed. Other defendants also had long criminal records. One had had fifteen gambling arrests over the past thirty years, eight of which had resulted in convictions. During the period of police observation at the Imperial Social Club, this same defendant was arrested on two separate occasions. He was fined two hundred and fifty dollars the first time, but only one hundred and fifty dollars the second time. Subsequently he was arrested three more times on gambling charges, with similar dispositions. One of the conclusions of the State Commission of Investigation, after its extensive analysis of these gambling prosecutions, was that the whole exercise was one of futility:

> It therefore seems clear that the large expenditure of man hours and manpower by police, district attorneys and the judiciary in the so-called enforcement of the gambling laws in New York City, from making surveillances to arrests and through all prosecutive actions and judicial proceedings, hardly justifies the inconsequential results that are obtained.

Surely, the sentences imposed, as illustrated in this report, are a travesty, and in no way deter illegal gambling activity. To the contrary, these court sentences appear to be nothing more than "licensing fees" to operate.

A new approach to gambling is plainly needed. Probably a Presidential Commission, or its equivalent, is the only practical means of bringing together all the conflicting considerations and developing an overall national policy to replace the unworkable and destructive system we have now.

PLEA BARGAINING

A lawyer talking to his client in a detention center in a major metropolitan area reported that he had worked out a deal so that the man could walk out of jail a free man. "If you plead guilty to petty larceny, the judge will sentence you to the eight months you have already been in jail," the lawyer coaxed.

"But I don't want to plead guilty to anything," the man said. "I'm innocent."

"Then you'll have to stay in jail for another five months until your case is reached for trial," the lawyer responded with a shrug.

Being sentenced to "time served" is just another wrinkle in the practice known as "plea bargaining" that has sprung up in busy criminal courts around the country as a means of clearing the docket of the crushing load of cases. Plea bargaining means that the prosecutor and defense lawyer negotiate a plea of guilty to a lesser offense than the one charged against the defendant and agree on the length of the sentence that will be recommended to the judge. The judge indicates that he will not impose a greater sentence than the one agreed upon between counsel. It is then up to the defendant to decide whether to accept the deal that has been worked out for him or take his chances on trial. If he cannot make bail, it often works out that he serves more time if he attempts to prove his *innocence* than he would serve if he pleaded *guilty*.

"It is not *plea* bargaining, it's *sentence* bargaining," says Robert Kasanov, Chief of the Criminal Defense Branch of the New York Legal Aid Society. Mr. Kasanov is a vociferous opponent of plea bargaining, which he regards as a total perversion of the concept of justice and due process.

Many prosecutors defend the practice, however, as a practical necessity in the face of mounting numbers of criminal cases. Plea bargaining recently received approval from the Supreme Court of the United States. But the National Advisory Commission on Criminal Justice Standards and Goals subsequently recommended that the practice be phased out over a five-year period.

Plea bargaining is particularly troublesome when it involves a defendant held in custody before trial because he cannot raise enough money to be released on bail. After he has been in custody for several months an offer to let him be sentenced to the time he has already been in jail makes a total travesty of the whole process. Who wouldn't plead guilty under these circumstances—whether actually guilty or innocent?

Many factors are involved in overcoming the problems caused by overcrowding and delay in the criminal courts. Better management techniques to eliminate waste motion and promote efficiency is an important first step. Removing cases that do not belong in the criminal court pipeline is another. Bail reforms are long overdue, as are speedy trial rules and greater use of alternatives to the traditional prosecutive chain. The answer is not simply more judges and more courtrooms. Making more sensible use of what we have is the real challenge.

Chapter 8

The Law Enforcement
Establishment

DISTRICT Attorney Frank Hogan likes to recount that one of the first courts established by Europeans on American soil was the "Worshipful Court of the Schout, Burgomeister and Scheppens," founded in New Amsterdam in 1653, during the period of Dutch colonization. The first schout—a combination constable, court clerk and prosecutor—was Joachim Pieterson Kuyter. Shortly after filing his certificate of election, Schout Kuyter was scalped by a Pachami Indian. Americans have reflected pretty much the same feeling toward law enforcement officials ever since, and often with good reason.

The policeman and the prosecutor are critical elements in the quest for justice. No one is in a more sensitive position when it comes to how the law is enforced. These law enforcement officials largely control who is to be arrested and prosecuted, what charges are to be filed and whether due-process guarantees are to be respected. If they are corrupt or incompetent or lazy, justice will fail.

Across the country today the resources of law enforcement are a shambles. Literally thousands of different agencies operate at various levels of government, usually in a totally uncoordinated and inefficient manner that neutralizes whatever good they might otherwise do. Law enforcement, in fact, is one of the most disorganized of all governmental functions. The present confusion is largely traceable to the natural growth and evolution of an institution that once depended entirely on volunteers and now depends primarily on underpaid, undertrained police officers and politically ambitious prosecuting attorneys.

THE POLICEMAN

The first recorded anticrime machinery was created by Alfred the Great, who reigned in England between 870 and 901 A.D. The original format was a mutual pledge system established among groups of ten families, known as "tithings," in which each member was responsible for raising a "hue and cry" to summon the others' help in catching persons who committed crimes. Making an arrest was rewarded; permitting an escape was subject to a fine. The tithings were organized in turn into "hundreds," and the "hundreds" were formed into "shires." To insure that the individual citizens performed their mutual pledge obligations, a "shire-reave" was appointed with overall supervisory responsibility, and "constables" were assigned each hundred to supply needed weapons and equipment. (Centuries later, the "shire-reave" evolved into the "Sheriff" of Wild West fame, a title which continues to exist in many sections of the country.)

During the reign of Edward I in the thirteenth century, the first official police forces were established as the "watch and ward" in larger English towns. The criminal law enforcement system continued to develop with the appointment of "justices of the peace," who performed both enforcement and judicial functions. Over a period of time, citizen volunteers were replaced by salaried police officers, as wealthier individuals began to hire substitutes to perform their assigned police duties. Unfortunately, paid police work did not attract especially well qualified candidates, and the general level of the police was little better than that of the criminals they were supposed to catch. The principal duty of the paid police officers was to walk the streets of the towns at night calling out, "All is well."

The industrial revolution transformed England from a predominantly rural to a predominantly urban society in a very brief time. Thousands of families moved into factory towns to find work. Police offices were established in various sections of the larger cities, operating independently in their particular geographical areas. Then came a major innovation to reduce crime—introduction of the gas streetlamp. In 1822, England's new Home Secretary, Sir Robert Peel, persuaded Parliament to enact legislation that would create a Metropolitan Police Force, patterned along the lines of a military unit, whose members would be required to wear a regular uniform. The organized force proved so effective that the concept soon spread to other parts of England and Europe. The policemen themselves were nicknamed "Bobbies," in honor of their originator.

Law enforcement in America was originally based on the English model, transplanted to the colonies in the seventeenth and eighteenth centuries. Following the American Revolution, however, sheriffs and constables were no longer appointed, but were instead elected by the people as a reaction against royal abuses. Thus began the pattern of partisan politics in law enforcement which continues to plague it today.

The earliest police forces in America consisted primarily of watchmen who patrolled the streets at night while the citizens slept. In New York City, this body was referred to as the "rattlewatch" because of the wooden rattles which they sounded as they made their rounds to reassure homeowners (and warn burglars) of their approach. Daytime police shifts were soon added as industrialization arrived. Eventually came the unified police departments; from their copper badges the nickname "cop" evolved. By the 1870's, most large cities had full-time police forces. Salary levels were low and public attitudes ranged from indifference to disrespect, with the result that recruiting capable officers was a chronic problem. The intrusion of pol-

itics into the administration of police departments—through
the election of those who ran them, or those who authorized
the funds to pay salaries—became a growing concern, producing
frequent calls for police reform. One person who made his
reputation from reorganizing and reforming police work was
future president Theodore Roosevelt, who, among other things,
hired the first woman in the New York Police Department.

From the beginning, law enforcement has been considered
primarily a function of *local* government, with the idea of state
involvement never really having taken hold. Most state police
primarily handle traffic offenses. The Federal role developed
almost accidentally out of the need to meet special enforcement
needs in collecting customs duties and taxes. The first Federal
law enforcement agency was the Revenue Cutter Service, established in 1789 to prevent smuggling. In 1836, the Postmaster
General was authorized to hire special employees to protect the
mails. Eventually other enforcement needs led to the creation
of additional special investigative units. The first group of general criminal investigators in the Federal government was a
force of twenty-five detectives authorized by Congress in 1868.
In 1924, the Federal Bureau of Investigation was organized
in the Department of Justice, under the direction of J. Edgar
Hoover. Other Federal investigative agencies became increasingly professionalized to deal with enforcement problems in
counterfeiting, immigration violations, income tax evasion, agri-
culture frauds and narcotics smuggling. In recent years, Federal
enforcement agencies have been strengthened and given broader
responsibilities. The primary responsibility for enforcing the
criminal laws, however, still rests with local units of government. Federal jurisdiction is limited to what has been expressly
enacted by Congress, and even today this is a very small portion
of overall criminal law enforcement.

Against this background it is no wonder that in 1967 the
Katzenbach Commission counted some 40,000 separate law
enforcement agencies in the United States on the Federal, state
and local levels. The Federal government accounts for 50 separate units, state governments for another 200, while the bulk

of law enforcement agencies are dispersed among local units of government—3,700 cities, 3,050 counties and 33,000 boroughs, towns and villages. Responsibility for enforcing the law, therefore, is extremely decentralized, with little coordination or direction, and many police functions are duplicated wastefully. Moreover, the capability level of most local police units is so low that they cannot possibly cope with serious crime problems. Despite repeated cries for improvements and reform, the quality of police personnel continues to be disappointing. Salaries are low. In-service training is spotty. Pride in the uniform is rare. Integrity problems exist in most large police departments. The National Advisory Commission on Criminal Justice Standards and Goals recently proposed that all police departments with fewer than ten—89 percent of the total—be consolidated with other units to promote efficiency.

The interrelationship of police resources and effectiveness in preventing crime is clear and direct. During World War II, when the German occupation government arrested the entire police force in Copenhagen, Denmark, citizen groups established vigilante teams in an effort to maintain law and order. With no regular police investigative force functioning in the city, crimes such as larceny and burglary, which do not involve much risk of possible identification by the victims, increased ten times. The level of street crimes, which could be prosecuted on the testimony of individual victims, remained essentially unchanged. As criminals realized that there was little chance of anyone tracking them down for committing crimes which could be achieved by stealth, however, they indulged themselves to the limit.

Successful police work must be swift, efficient and effective. This means adequate personnel, equipment and support resources, productive but fair investigative and arrest procedures and, above all, strong backup from prosecutors and courts in bringing arrested persons promptly to trial. Unfortunately, we are still a long way from achieving these objectives.

A 1972 report by the Committee for Economic Development, entitled "Reducing Crime and Assuring Justice," placed principal responsibility for ineffective police work on the state governments:

> The main constitutional responsibility for crime prevention and control rests upon the states, an assignment they have botched. They have failed to keep their criminal codes up-to-date, and they have turned responsibility for enforcement over to a welter of overlapping counties, municipalities, townships, and special districts. Despite the obvious and urgent need, the states have neither straightened out their tangled and ineffective patterns of local government nor assumed direct responsibility for law enforcement.

To a large extent the same criticisms can also be made about Federal law enforcement. Congress simply has not met its responsibilities. Although certain Federal agencies (notably the FBI) have received generous financial support from Congress, other agencies have been starved for money and personnel. As of 1972, the Securities and Exchange Commission, which has primary jurisdiction to investigate securities fraud and protect the investing public against abuses and criminal misconduct, had fewer employees nationwide than it had in 1940. There were only 1,403 employees of the SEC in all, ranging from the Commission's chairman to the building guards. In contrast, there were 4,000 broker-dealers to be monitored, plus hundreds of thousands of individual transactions, as well as numerous investment advisors and investment companies. In the New York City regional office, which covers Wall Street's financial operations, there were only 139 SEC employees, from file clerks to investigators and lawyers. In the same region there were 2,136 broker-dealers, 500 mutual funds, and 1,700 investment advisors. With the existing manpower, the SEC had the capability to conduct a regular audit of investment companies only once every 17 years. The total salaries of the New York Stock Exchange alone are double that of the entire payroll of the SEC *nationwide.*

Similar shortages have existed in the Internal Revenue Service, where only a handful of audits can be performed each year out of the millions of tax returns that are filed. Because of congressional criticisms in past years, together with a number of scandals, the IRS has become quite muscle-bound in many of its procedures, and its enforcement efficiency is therefore only a fraction of what it might be.

The most obvious unmet need in the law enforcement establishment is intelligent planning and strategy on how to make the most effective use of police resources to *prevent* crime. A spirit of professionalism is obviously an important part of this objective and incorporates the need for good pay, high admission standards, and continuing in-service training and education. Intelligence-gathering and creative planning, however, are equally important and with few exceptions have so far been achieved, if at all, largely by chance. Imaginative senior enforcement officials are rare. Most ranking police officials reach their positions of command through length of service, and usually because they have not rocked the boat.

Some way must be found to discourage the promotion of those with "cop mentalities" to positions of leadership. Bright, capable, creative people are urgently needed to help in the strategic allocation of resources where they will do the most good in fair and effective law enforcement. There is a deep-seated conviction among most police officials that the only people who can enforce the law are detective types. Lawyers, they feel, must stick to legal research and arguing cases, and everyone else had better stay out of the way. This shortsighted approach is one of the reasons why law enforcement agencies have so frequently proved totally inadequate to deal with modern problems of criminal justice. There is room today for management specialists, engineers, social workers, economists and a wide range of experts and research technicians to help enforce the law effectively and more sensibly. New thinking about the structure and operation of police agencies is long overdue.

THE PROSECUTOR

On the wall of the courtroom in the Nelson County Courthouse in Lovingston, Virginia, hangs a portrait of a handsome

white-haired lawyer standing in a relaxed pose with his hands
thrust deep into his pockets. Underneath the painting is a brass
plate identifying the subject as Robert Whitehead, who once
served as the Commonwealth Attorney for the county. Then
follows this tribute: "There stands old Bob Whitehead, as usual
with his hands in his pockets. I never saw them in anyone
else's."

This testimony to the integrity of a local prosecuting attorney
is both delightful and disturbing. Why should we be surprised
when a prosecuting attorney turns out to be honest?

Under the American system of justice, the prosecuting attorney has emerged as the chief law enforcement officer. The
citizenry and press look to him to take action when a crime
wave hits. Investigations into public corruption and misconduct
are his responsibility. He must propose legislative changes, act
as law enforcement spokesman for the community and issue
statements about problems of crime and its prevention. His ability to fulfill this responsibility is a key determinant of the success
or failure of a law enforcement program. Because of the manner
of his selection, usually through the political process, the odds
are against having a prosecutor in office who can perform all
of his functions well. Too often the men who are selected are
incompetent, and sometimes they are overreaching or venal.
Many prosecutors have limited staff, limited professional knowledge and training and, most disturbing of all, little interest in
their jobs except as political stepping-stones to higher public
office.

The prosecuting attorney is expected to be relatively detached
in the handling of criminal cases, representing the community's
interest in justice and fair play as much as his own interest in
bringing law violators to book. He has a responsibility, for
example, to unearth evidence that negates the guilt of the accused and to make it available to the defense. Unlike other
lawyers, be cannot think in terms first of winning or losing.
His job is not to convict, but to see that justice is done.

Generally speaking, prosecutors count on the police and other
official investigative agencies to look into whatever crimes come

to their attention, assemble the evidence and make the arrests. But there are many areas of criminal conduct which do not ordinarily show up through complaints to the police and where some searching out must be done. This is particularly true in fields such as official corruption, organized and white-collar crime. Here is where the prosecutor can play his most important role in the investigation of crime and its prevention. But to do so he must have knowledge of the principal areas of criminal conduct. In addition, he should have sources of broad intelligence information sufficient to plan strategy, and he ought to have the experience and ingenuity to be able to use the limited resources available to him most effectively in conducting difficult investigations. The prosecuting attorney should not be passive in his approach to his duties, waiting for the cases to come to him. Instead, he should take an active, affirmative role in investigating significant areas of illegal conduct that might otherwise never come before the courts—misfeasance in government, victimization of the poor, business crime, damage to the environment.

A prosecuting attorney under our system has tremendous power, and with that power there is the potential for abuse. Particularly when a prosecutor is politically ambitious and thinks of his office as the road to the governorship or other high elected position, the temptation to seek personal publicity out of the functions of the office can be very real. Abuse of the office begins to creep in when a prosecutor makes decisions based on his own personal stake in the publicity that might result. Publicity-seeking is one of the chronic potential abuses in prosecutors' offices. This becomes particularly serious where a grand jury investigation is involved. Press leaks as to who is being summoned before a grand jury may produce good newspaper copy, but they can also do irreparable harm to the person who has been called to testify. In the minds of most citizens, being called before a grand jury is tantamount to being accused of wrongdoing. Since the grand jury proceedings are secret, there is no way a witness can properly defend himself. The newsworthiness of the person summoned before the grand jury can generate even larger headlines. The only proper rule is complete secrecy as to the identity of all grand jury witnesses.

Another obvious area of potential abuse by prosecuting attorneys is that of political favoritism. Political influence can affect the selection of the prosecutor's staff. Such influence can be employed to protect political allies from investigations and prosecutions, diverting the prosecutor's resources to harrassment of people in the opposing party.

What should we expect of the prosecuting attorney? He should be independent and generously endowed with common sense. He should have a broad knowledge of societal problems and needs. He should be vigorous, inventive and courageous. The most important factor in achieving these goals is the selection process. Reforms similar to those in the selection process for judges should be implemented. Merit should take precedence over political considerations. Prosecutors should be nominated by the governor after prior approval of the candidate by a screening committee which includes lay members. Appointments should require legislative confirmation following a public hearing. Where feasible, prosecutors should be appointed on a regional basis. The media should serve as the public's watchdog against abuses in the selection process.

ENFORCEMENT POLICY

Each May 1 is "Law Day" by proclamation of the President of the United States. In 1973, the President's action in setting aside May 1 as a day of observance in honor of law and justice was particularly ironic. The morning newspapers of Law Day 1973 carried screaming headlines reporting the resignations of the Attorney General of the United States, the Counsel to the President of the United States and two top presidential aides, submitted in the wake of widening disclosures of top-level involvement in one of the most notorious cases of illegal electronic eavesdropping in history—the Watergate scandal. What added to the irony was that the President and his Administration had gone into office as advocates of "law and order." Throughout the preceding four and a half years of management of the Executive Branch, the President and many of his cabinet officers had consistently stressed new programs of law enforcement: a crackdown on organized crime; expanded resources for prosecuting narcotics traffic; new programs to provide financial aid to local law enforcement agencies. Any casual observer would have concluded that there was strong national leadership for vigorous enforcement of the law. But the Watergate disclosures proved otherwise—that Federal law enforcement policy at the top was two-faced: one policy for muggers, mobsters and narcotics pushers; another policy for friends and insiders. The very machinery of justice that was designed to enforce the law was used to cover up crimes, destroy incriminating evidence and silence witnesses.

The Watergate affair revealed an ethical bankruptcy at the very place where it could do the greatest harm to enforcement policy, staff morale and public confidence. As a result, it will be many years before the American public will again put full trust in the impartiality and fairness of the Federal Government's enforcement of the law.

The very first qualification for appointment to high Federal office is integrity. In fact, the wording of every presidential commission begins with these words: "KNOW YE, That reposing special trust and confidence in the *Integrity,* Ability and Learning of . . ."

Even prior to Watergate, there was a series of incidents which had shaken public confidence in the integrity of government. Over the course of two or three years citizens were subjected to one jolt after another as persons in positions of high public trust were unmasked as dishonest.

An Associate Justice of the Supreme Court of the United States was forced to resign following disclosures of improper relationships for personal gain with a convicted stock swindler.

The Administrative Assistant to the Speaker of the House

of Representatives was convicted for committing perjury before a Grand Jury investigating misuse of the powers of the Speaker's Office on behalf of a notorious influence peddler.

The Administrative Assistant to a United States Senator was convicted in connection with a bribe attempt to fix an SEC investigation through the Deputy Attorney General of the United States.

A judge of the United States Court of Appeals for the Seventh Circuit, former Governor of Illinois and once-respected chairman of a national commission investigating civil disorders, was indicted, convicted and sentenced to three years in prison for improper financial gains in connection with favored treatment given to a racetrack owner.

These instances of lack of integrity in positions of public trust had been disheartening, but with each new disclosure there was at least one positive note: Thank Heaven there was a Federal law-enforcement machinery which was incorruptible and scrupulous in ferreting out wrongdoing and prosecuting wrongdoers.

Then came the greatest shock of all—or series of shocks, for they seemed never-ending—attacks on the integrity of the United States Department of Justice, the Federal Bureau of Investigation and top White House aides. The original facts largely came from actions or published statements by the participants themselves:

The Acting Director of the FBI resigned in the face of public disclosures that he had destroyed incriminating documents delivered to him by the White House.

One former Attorney General of the United States publicly admitted knowledge of discussions centering on the possibility of committing a Federal crime of the most distasteful sort.

His successor as Attorney General disqualified himself from supervising an expanding investigation into that crime because of his personal relationship with those who might be implicated, and subsequently resigned.

Repeated public references were made to involvement of White House staff members, not only in the crime itself, but, even worse, in the attempt to cover up afterward. Three top presidential aides resigned in the wake of these disclosures.

The question of legal culpability in such a situation is one for grand juries and the courts, but there is another aspect of the whole sorry business that should be openly discussed: that is, the damage that is done to the public's confidence in the integrity of the administration of justice and enforcement of law on the Federal level when there is any doubt as to the sincerity, motivation or honesty of those who are in top leadership positions. When those who run the principal Federal investigative agency, the Department of Justice and many programs in the White House itself are under suspicion, then all enforcement officials who are striving to uphold standards of integrity are also made suspect. The effectiveness of law enforcement itself is bound to suffer. When a handful of willful men make a mockery of the concept of honest government, as was done in the Watergate incident and its aftermath, a shadow is cast on all who are involved in the administration of justice —judges, public defenders, prosecutors, investigative agencies and the hundreds of thousands of career civil servants who dedicate their productive working years to the hazards of police work, the burdens of court administration, the frequent heartbreak of probation, parole and correction work and the tedium of the countless clerical tasks that are essential to ensuring a fair and impartial government of law.

Shortly before George Washington took the first oath of office as President of the United States, he wrote the following words to Alexander Hamilton:

"I hope I shall always possess firmness and virtue enough to maintain the character of an honest man."

Firmness and virtue are the essential ingredients of integrity in government. That integrity means honor, forthrightness and incorruptibility as a matter of personal habit and conviction.

It does not mean simply not violating the law.

It does not mean simply not accepting bribes.

It does not mean simply not telling lies.

It means, rather, something much more positive—the moral

strength to always do what one knows in one's heart is the right thing to do; the moral strength to act promptly and forcefully to prevent others from doing what one knows is wrong; the moral strength to make impartial judgments without fear or favor.

All of us have the basic seeds of integrity within us, but cultivating them requires two additional elements: personal training and discipline, and leadership from one's peers and superiors.

It is this second element of leadership in integrity that was lost through the Watergate affair. Those who should have been providing that leadership instead set examples of deception and concealment. People in high places destroyed important documents, dealt in large amounts of secret cash and withheld information about possible violation of Federal laws; and some, at least, may have actually participated in the commission of an ugly crime that strikes at the heart of fair play in the elective process.

Whether public officials, lawyers, or just plain citizens, the rest of us should not sit quietly by when questions are raised as to the conduct of officials in law-enforcement policy-making positions. It is not enough that any crimes themselves be investigated and the guilty prosecuted. What is even more important is that the basic fiber of national leadership must be strengthened. If enforcement of the law is to comply with proper standards of justice, officials must be found in whom the public can have unquestioned confidence—leaders selected on merit rather than partisanship, on ability rather than political loyalty and, above all, on the basis of clearly demonstrated personal integrity. To avoid future Watergates, enforcement policy must be set and carried out by professionals who are far removed from political machinery and whose commitment and independence are beyond question.

CONSTITUTIONAL RIGHTS

No freeman shall be taken, or imprisoned, or disseized, or outlawed, or exiled, or in any way harmed, nor will we go upon or send upon him, save by the lawful judgment of his peers or by the law of the land.

These were important words when they were written into the Magna Carta in 1215. They spelled the beginning of "due process of law," which has evolved over the years into a set of basic rules guaranteeing fairness in the way we prosecute criminal cases. We have translated those rules into the Bill of Rights to the United States Constitution:

> The right of the people to be secure in their persons, houses, papers, and effects against unreasonable searches and seizures shall not be violated, and no warrants shall issue but upon probable cause, supported by oath or affirmation, and particularly describing the place to be searched and the persons or things to be seized.
>
> *—Fourth Amendment*

> No person shall be held to answer for a capital, or otherwise infamous crime, unless on a presentment or indictment of a Grand Jury; nor shall any person be subject for the same offense to be twice put in jeopardy of life or limb; nor shall be compelled in any criminal case to be a witness against himself, nor be deprived of life, liberty, or property, without due process of law; . . .
>
> *—Fifth Amendment*

> In all criminal prosecutions, the accused shall enjoy the right to a speedy and public trial, by an impartial jury of the State and district wherein the crime shall have been committed, which district shall have been previously ascertained by law, and to be informed of the nature and cause of the accusation; to be confronted with the witnesses against him; to have compulsory process for obtaining witnesses in his favor, and to have the assistance of counsel for his defense.
>
> *—Sixth Amendment*

> Excessive bail shall not be required, nor excessive fines imposed, nor cruel and unusual punishments inflicted.
>
> *—Eighth Amendment*

> . . . nor shall any state . . . deny to any person within its jurisdiction the equal protection of the laws.
>
> *—Fourteenth Amendment*

Law enforcement officials have accused the United States Supreme Court of "handcuffing the police" in the application of these constitutional rights in recent cases. The decisions of the Warren Court in the *Escobedo*, *Mapp*, *Miranda* and *Gideon* cases are widely cited by police and prosecutors as excuses for ineffective law enforcement. Such arguments are, of course, largely nonsense. There is nothing truly inhibiting about the application of these constitutional guarantees. They may create inconvenience, but they do not prevent meaningful law enforcement. Though some of the *remedies* have proved to be poorly thought through and ineffective, the goals themselves are proper ones.

The key to sound implementation of constitutional rights is common sense. Unfortunately, too many people tend to discuss civil liberties with no understanding of how law enforcement procedures really work, so that their approach tends to be emotional rather than rational. Much of the public discussion about constitutional rights in America is characterized by fuzzy thinking on the part of civil libertarians who claim to be keepers of the public conscience. Far more progress could be made in giving practical significance and application to the Bill of Rights if those who serve as self-appointed watchdogs over law enforcement machinery had a better understanding of how that machinery functioned.

Part of the problem is a communications block when it comes to discussing questions of constitutional rights with people in law enforcement. Seldom is a law enforcement officer invited to participate in civil rights conferences or other public discussions of problems of trial procedure, use of grand juries, interrogation of suspects or the like. This is unfortunate because there are so many truly decent people in law enforcement who are acutely aware of their constitutional obligations and who would welcome an opportunity to discuss them openly with people who challenge law enforcement techniques. But instead, such discussions are usually carried on in a vacuum by people who essentially do not know what they are talking about. All sorts of false assumptions are made as to the practices followed by law enforcement agencies, with total ignorance of the practicalities of collecting evidence, questioning witnesses and the psychology of guilty defendants or cooperating witnesses. Better input to these discussions would produce much more useful results. Instead, the discussions of constitutional rights are usually entirely academic, and the positions taken are so extreme and removed from reality that they have no practical impact at all.

One perfect example of this type of know-nothing approach was a public attack launched by the New York Civil Liberties Union criticizing public hearings held by the Knapp Commission, which was then investigating police corruption in New York City. The Knapp Commission itself had operated with unusual fairness in conducting its investigations, and was administered by experienced people with knowledge both of defendants' rights and of practical law enforcement needs. The Civil Liberties Union, without bothering to think about what it was saying, rushed into print on October 24, 1971, with a statement in *The New York Times* which condemned everything in sight:

> We are opposed to trial by public exposure, electronic surveillance, the use of undercover agents without judicial approval, the use of inherently unreliable informer testimony, and entrapment.

All the words had a ring of righteousness to them, but the substance was nonexistent. There was no "trial by public exposure"—the Commission had very carefully prohibited any references to the names of police officers about whom testimony was given, and witnesses referred to them by letters of the alphabet, so that no public charges were made against individuals; instead, the hearings focused on the *system* that was corrupt. There was no "electronic surveillance," only the use of recording devices during specific conversations to guarantee that discoveries made by investigators working undercover were fully corroborated before being brought before the public. Such use of recording equipment with the consent of one party to a conversation has been fully approved by the Supreme Court. The opposition to the "use of undercover agents without judicial approval" reflected incredible ignorance of the law enforcement process. Virtually every significant investigation involves some form of undercover work, whether it is the surveillance of a meeting, or the purchase by a narcotics agent of heroin from a pusher. Judicial approval would not affect the fairness of such investigative techniques, which are always open to attack during any subsequent criminal proceeding, but would only have the effect of tying up the already overcrowded courts with thousands of applications for no practical purpose. The reference to testimony by witnesses under oath as "inherently unreliable informer testimony" was probably the most foolish statement of all. In virtually every crime, and particularly cases involving corruption, truly reliable testimony as to what happened can be given *only* by the direct participants. Calling them "informers" is both inaccurate and misleading. By definition, an informer is one who provides information and investigative leads, not direct testimony, and almost invariably he is kept under wraps, not put on the witness stand. As for "entrapment," there was no suggestion whatsoever that any police officer referred to in the Knapp hearings had been enticed or persuaded into engaging in corrupt actions which he would otherwise not have performed—the legal test for entrapment. Quite to the contrary, the public hearings disclosed an eagerness by police officers to engage in corrupt practices at every opportunity.

Such reckless public attacks by the supposed guardians of our constitutional liberties hurt those liberties by demonstrating to sensible people that the guardians do not know what they are talking about. If we are really to have effective supervision over the fairness of our criminal justice system, we need watchers who understand the way the courts work and the difference between fair and unfair methods in the law enforcement process.

One good example of the problems that can develop from muddled thinking is the "exclusionary rule" now widely followed in state and Federal criminal proceedings. A series of Supreme Court decisions have held inadmissable evidence obtained through searches and seizures in violation of the Fifth and Sixth Amendments, improperly obtained identification testimony or evidence obtained by methods which violate the due process clause of the Fifth Amendment. The main rationale behind excluding evidence which violates any of these rights is that such exclusion will serve as a method of discipling law enforcement officers and thereby have a therapeutic effect. But nothing in our experience under the exclusionary rule supports this theory. If anything, the exclusion of otherwise valid evidence has made something of a mockery of the whole judicial process and has provided law enforcement officers with a scapegoat, the Supreme Court.

The test on exclusion of evidence should really turn on whether the evidence is reliable or not. In many cases, violations of constitutional guarantees will in fact cast doubt on the reliability of the evidence itself, as when a suspect has been held for a long period of time and questioned extensively before he has made a confession. Improper identification procedures may also compromise the reliability of identification testimony. Obviously such evidence should be excluded because it may not reflect the truth. But when it comes to objective physical evidence obtained during the course of an improper search and seizure, no question of reliability ordinarily exists. In such cases, the sole reason for exclusion is to punish the wayward police officer. But is that really what happens? Is it not really society that is being punished, while the police officer is simply bemused at the ridiculous result?

Thoughtful people have suggested that more effective techniques should be utilized to discipline law enforcement officers who fail to comply with constitutional guarantees. Such techniques might include judicial censure of the offending officer, which could be placed in his personnel file and affect future promotions. The techniques could even include the imposition of some form of monetary penalty, to be paid out of the officer's own pocket. Such sanctions would be meaningful, while excluding the evidence is not.

Where a violation of a constitutional right has been so extreme as to shock one's sense of fair play, then a case might be made for exclusion on the ground that the court system should not be party to unfair practices. But where the illegality of the search and seizure turns on some technicality, such as a procedural defect, then exclusion of the evidence becomes primarily an injustice to society.

Ironically, the exclusionary rule has itself become an instrument of corruption in the court system. Detectives who are bribed to fix narcotics cases prefer to do so in connection with hearings on motions to suppress evidence, where a very small change in testimony can produce a technical defect in the execution of the search warrant and can automatically result in the judge throwing out the evidence, and with it the case. In such situations, rather than penalize the police officer who ostensibly violated the defendant's rights, the exclusionary rule has proven to be a bonanza for the crooked policeman.

Wiretapping is another area that consistently draws an emotional response, usually based on total ignorance of the real facts. Many people still oppose the use of wiretaps despite statutory authorization permitting their use in a limited group of criminal investigations. The irony is that, operating under the present statute, there is absolutely no chance of casual eavesdropping on private conversations of innocent citizens on the part of law enforcement officers. The risk comes from *illegal*, not *legal*, wiretapping.

Statutory limitations on the use of Federal wiretaps are far stricter than those covering the making of arrests or the issuing of search warrants. A court order must be obtained in advance, based on a full set of papers establishing probable cause. The order is limited to fifteen days, and every five days the investigating agency must report its findings to the judge who authorized the wiretap so that he can satisfy himself that probable cause was in fact justified. The telephone subscriber must be given written notice of the interception within ninety days, and all papers relating to the wiretap order must be turned over to the defendant if a prosecution is thereafter instituted on the basis of intercepted calls. On top of these stringent requirements, a heavy commitment of manpower is required to properly transcribe notes and report back findings to the judge, making wiretapping a very expensive investigative technique of only limited applicability. The number of wiretaps that have in fact been authorized under the legislation have been remarkably few, and most have been related almost entirely to investigations of organized crime.

Not all wiretapping provides a basis for prosecuting and convicting people. William M. Tendy, former Chief of the Narcotics Unit in the U. S. Attorney's office for the Southern District of New York, testified before the House Select Committee on Crime in 1970 that the use of a wiretap in a narcotics smuggling case convinced the prosecutor's office that two of the five people who had been under suspicion were in fact innocent, and cases against them were dismissed. All of which goes to show that there are some significant things to be said on both sides of civil liberties issues, but most of the time nobody bothers to consider them. As a result, many abuses go uncorrected, while many legitimate law enforcement functions are unnecessarily restricted.

Chapter 9

The Correction System: Unwitting Partner in Crime

WHEN he was nineteen years old, Nat Caldwell was arrested for first-degree murder in connection with a street fight in the Bedford-Stuyvesant section of Brooklyn. A man had been killed with a .25-caliber automatic pistol which Caldwell later admitted belonged to him. The incident appeared to be the last downhill slide in the decline of a young black who had started out life as a bright boy in the local parochial school. Nat's father had abandoned his mother when he was still very young, and she had been forced to go on welfare. There was no more money for parochial school, so the boy was transferred to public school where he found himself far ahead of his classmates in school work. Boredom set in, and then truancy. By the time he was seventeen, Nat had dropped out of school. He mostly hung around the neighborhood drinking wine with his buddies, also dropouts. (This was before drugs swept through the area.) Nat enlisted in the Marine Corps in hopes of finding a new life, but soon he was AWOL from the kitchen job to which he was assigned, and then he was court-martialed. After two more court-martials, Caldwell received a bad conduct discharge and was soon back on the streets of Bedford-Stuyvesant hanging around with the old crowd (who by now had turned to marijuana). Twenty-eight days later he was under arrest.

Caldwell maintained that he did not fire the gun that killed the man during the street fight, but his court-assigned lawyer told him that he would be convicted of first-degree murder anyway if he stood trial. After almost a year in the Brooklyn House of Detention, Nat agreed to plead guilty to second-degree manslaughter. He was sentenced to five-to-ten years in Auburn State Prison.

With his background, being sent to Auburn should have been the final blow in a wasted life. But it was not. Today Caldwell is Manhattan Borough Director for the Vera Institute's Court Employment Project, responsible for supervising a large staff and the expenditure of over a million dollars a year. What made the change defied every rule of experience and common sense.

When Caldwell first arrived at the Brooklyn House of Detention he promised himself he would never come back. Then, when he was sent to Auburn Prison, he set out on a plan to rehabilitate himself. He took a Dale Carnegie course and practiced it on his fellow inmates. He sent away for self-improvement books and read them from cover to cover. He earned his high school equivalency diploma and became an instructor in the prison school. He served as a counselor to inmates who had personal problems and helped them write letters home. When he emerged from prison he was a new man. Not because of what the prison had taught him, but rather in spite of it.

Nat Caldwell now believes that a few basic changes in prison policy and administration could salvage the majority of prisoners who are sent away. Eliminating the prison "underworld" is one important step, along with turning the skills which are wasted on illegal pursuits in prison to constructive alternatives. Caldwell advocates a total overhaul of the parole system, which, he says, places a premium on deception and double-dealing. Most important, Caldwell believes that inmates themselves can provide the cadre for a truly workable rehabilitation program, even for high-security institutions, at very little additional cost. The problem is that no one is listening to Nat Caldwell and people like him, and as a result our prisons are in a state of crisis.

THE LESSONS OF ATTICA

Shortly after 9:00 A.M. on September 9, 1971, a young prison guard stationed at "Times Square," the gate at the intersection of two long tunnels which divide Attica State Prison's huge courtyard, observed two groups of inmates running in his direction. The guard was twenty-eight-year-old Billy Quinn, a thin-faced, clean-cut man who was well liked by most of the prisoners. As the inmates rushed it, a weakened bolt in the gate gave way. Quinn's crumpled body was later found lying on the floor. With his skull fractured in two places, the injured guard was turned over to prison authorities by one of the inmate leaders. Two days later, Billy Quinn died—the first of a series of senseless deaths in the bloodiest prison uprising of this century.

The most important result of the Attica Prison riot was its shock effect on the American conscience. For years, prisons had operated in a world unto themselves, with no supervision or guidance from anyone else in the criminal justice system. Prosecutors and judges had taken the position that their responsibility ended with conviction. Government officials and legislators looked on prison reform as an unpopular issue with the electorate, which generally opposes the "coddling" of prisoners. And so it was left to the prison administrators, brought up in the tradition of security and punishment as the ends of the process, to run the correction system.

Four months after Attica, Arch E. Sayler, former Chief Probation Officer of the Federal court in Manhattan, told a group of lawyers:

> I hope the day will come when we in the United States are mature enough to deal with offenders, not as discards, but as a recoverable commodity. We are learning to recycle our natural resources, and we already know a great deal about how to recycle people, but we prefer to continue making the same old mistakes over and over again. I believe this is because we, as a people, get some kind of evil satisfaction

out of making other people scapegoats. We are reluctant to change our old habits.

The "old habits" to which Mr. Sayler referred are steeped in a history that has been pretty grim. Believe it or not, sending criminals to prison was regarded as a humanitarian procedure when it was first inaugurated in the late eighteenth century. Before that, the form of punishment tended to "fit the crime." The hands of the thief were cut off, the tongue of the perjurer was torn out, the rapist was castrated. In 1786, Quakers in Pennsylvania advocated imprisonment as a humane alternative to such raw forms of punishment. The original concept of prisons was that criminals should be locked up in small solitary cells so that they could do penance for their sins. The first warden of the Maine State Prison expressed the view that prisons should be "dark and comfortless abodes of guilt and wretchedness."

The first wave of reform to hit the prison system came in 1825, when New York State's Auburn Prison introduced hard labor as a means of providing diversion from the boredom of solitary confinement, which had often led to insanity or early death. The "Auburn System," which also included security lockups, shaved heads and lock-step marching, has largely continued down to recent times. Although there have been stirrings of reform from time to time, and a few significant experiments, prison officials have continued to emphasize the prevention of escapes and the keeping of prisoners "in line."

On a typical day, there are 1.3 million persons being processed by the nation's correction system. Approximately one-third of these are in correctional institutions, and the balance are under probation or parole supervision. During the year, about 2½ million persons enter into the correctional system either as first offenders or repeat violators.

Many people believe that community supervision holds the greatest hope for salvaging human beings who are convicted of crimes. There are other apparent advantages, one of which is economy—probation costs only one-sixth as much as institutionalization, and parole only one-fourteenth. But this may be a false economy. While two-thirds of the offenders in the correction system are on probation or parole, only one-third of the correction employees work in that field. The other two-thirds work in institutions. Probation and parole officers average about one hundred cases each, in contrast to the ideal goal of thirty-five cases or less. These officers have something like fifteen minutes per month available to do their supervisory work on each person in their care. Emphasis on the preparation of presentence reports for the courts uses up so much of the time of probation officers that their ability to supervise their case loads is even more limited than might appear from the raw statistics.

The main focus in corrections has been the correctional institutions themselves—the jails, prisons and other custodial facilities which house offenders awaiting trial or serving sentences. Most people think of prisons as places that should emphasize rehabilitation. According to a public opinion survey conducted for the Joint Commission on Correctional Manpower and Training, inquiring of adults what the main emphasis of prisons should be, 72 per cent named rehabilitation, 12 per cent chose protection of society and 7 per cent cited punishment. The remaining 9 per cent expressed no view. Teenagers questioned during the survey placed even greater emphasis on the rehabilitation role of correctional institutions, some 83 per cent affirming this as the purpose of imprisonment.

In sharp contrast with these noble hopes, the true picture of correctional institutions today is an ugly one indeed. A substantial number of inmates are housed in local jails, originally designed as temporary detention facilities for prisoners awaiting trial. A census of the nation's jail population conducted by the Law Enforcement Assistance Administration in 1970 disclosed that over one hundred and sixty thousand persons were being held in jail, a majority of whom had *not* been convicted of any crime. The number of jails across the country totaled over four thousand. Of the larger institutions, 86 per cent had no recreation facilities, 89 per cent had no educational facilities and 49 per cent had no medical facilities. Other jails lacked visiting facilities, were overcrowded, obsolete, and in a few cases even lacked toilets. "Jails are tanks—human warehouses," says Norman Carlson, Director of the Federal Bureau of Prisons. "Anyone not a criminal will be one when he gets out of jail."

Although theoretically better equipped to provide rehabilitation services, the record of the nation's prisons is not much better than that of the local jails. Chief Justice Warren E. Burger warned a meeting of the American Bar Association in 1970 that there were at least nine basic defects in the typical American prison:

1. Facilities tend to be old and inefficient.

2. Efforts at vocational training for inmates are frequently out of date and unrelated to the needs of the job market.

3. Professional medical and psychiatric services are in short supply.

4. Recreational facilities are scarce and limited.

5. Education and vocational training are generally nonexistent.

6. The concept of training through work release has received only limited and grudging acceptance.

7. Little progress has been made in developing facilities to help in the transition process from prison life to civilian life.

8. Research in correctional techniques and results is virtually nonexistent.

9. The salary scales for correctional personnel are too low to attract qualified people.

Observed the Chief Justice:

Do you know or can you conceive of an industrial enterprise with two hundred thousand employees, which turns out a critical product and would use fifty to one hundred-and-fifty-year-old plants, equipment and techniques, no research, low pay and little or no training for its production workers, no long-range planning, no concern for its output or quality control?

These deficiencies were largely restated in 1972 in the incisive official report of the commission that investigated the

Attica tragedy, which was ably headed by Robert B. McKay, Dean of New York University Law School.

One of the clear symptoms of trouble in correctional institutions has been the pattern of prison unrest. In a period of only four months at the end of 1971, the following series of uprisings left scores of persons injured and over fifty persons dead:

On August 21, three prisoners and three guards were killed in an apparent escape attempt at California State Prison, San Quentin.

Between September 9 and 13, eleven prison employees and thirty-two inmates were killed at the uprising at Attica.

On October 2, injuries were received by ten prison guards and eleven inmates during an uprising at the Illinois State Penitentiary in Pontiac, Illinois.

On October 4, three correction employees were injured and one inmate killed during a brief uprising at the Dallas County jail in Dallas, Texas.

On October 12, two hundred and fifty inmates staged a rebellion at the San Joaquin County jail, in Stockton, California.

On October 19, twenty-four inmates armed with iron pipes confronted forty guards in an uprising at Illinois State Penitentiary, Joliet, Illinois.

On November 6, one hundred and fifty prisoners seized a cell block at the Los Angeles Hall of Justice, in Los Angeles, California.

On November 7, one inmate was injured and another killed during a protest at the Kentucky State Prison, in Eddyville, Kentucky.

On November 12, one inmate and fifteen correction employees were injured during a prison disturbance at Wisconsin State Reformatory, in Green Bay, Wisconsin.

On November 16, one hundred inmates seized two hostages during a disturbance at the model New Jersey Correction Center, in Yardville, New Jersey.

On November 24 and 25, six guards and the warden were

held as hostages by some five hundred prisoners in an uprising at the New Jersey State Prison, in Rahway, New Jersey.

A number of factors have contributed to the unrest in the nation's prisons. One has been the bitterness of inmates who are acutely aware that unequal sentences are handed down for similar offenses. On top of this is a feeling that the criminal justice system is essentially racist, since the percentage of blacks in the inmate population totals nearly 40 per cent, more than three times the relative ratio of blacks in the overall population. To make matters worse, only 5 per cent of correction employees are black.

Another factor contributing to unrest among prisoners is the inadequate system for airing grievances. More and more, prisoners have pinned their hopes on the proliferation of court writs seeking redress for complaints related to unfair prison treatment or unfairness in the original adjudication process. Lack of adequate professional legal guidance in the preparation and processing of these petitions, however, has forced the courts to expend precious time trying to distinguish meritless applications from worthy ones, and has thus unwittingly slowed down the judicial process.

About 95 per cent of all offenders in the correction system are male, most of them between fifteen and thirty years old, and a substantial proportion of them coming from the urban slums, with economic, educational and other disadvantages. A study by the Manpower Administration of the U. S. Department of Labor found that over 54 per cent of those in prison have less than a high school education, in contrast to 34 per cent in the general population. Some 30 per cent of all inmates have completed one to four years of high school, in contrast to 48 per cent in the general population. Only 5 per cent of the prison population have attended college (1 per cent completing four years), in contrast to 18 per cent in the general population. Employment skills and experience show a comparable pattern of disadvantage: 60 per cent of those in prison have work experience as laborers, service workers or operatives, in comparison to 38 per cent in the overall general labor force. The need for extensive academic and vocational training to compensate for these disadvantages is self-evident.

The evidence that prisons do not successfully rehabilitate is overwhelming. The FBI reported in 1971 that of some sixteen thousand offenders who had been released to the community in the year 1965, 75 per cent had been arrested for another offense by the end of the fourth year following release. The rearrest rate for those who had been placed on probation, by contrast, was only 56 per cent. Obviously these figures are affected by the initial judicial determination that one offender was more suitable for probation than another, but still the 75 per cent rate of recidivism is not much of an endorsement of the prison system in rehabilitating those who are placed in its care.

What makes the failure of our present correction system particularly frustrating is the staggering cost to the taxpayer. The annual corrections budget is substantially more than one billion dollars. The money expended on corrections for any one individual violator during his lifetime can be considerable. The District of Columbia Corrections Department made a study of the total correction costs for 25 young men paroled from the District of Columbia's Youth Center in 1968. The men had a median age of 26 years and had spent an average of 32 months in the Youth Center, plus 8.5 months in Federal reformatories, 4.5 months in the District of Columbia jail, 23 months on parole, 2 months on probation, 16 months in welfare institutions, 22 months in foster homes and 6 months on juvenile probation. During the average 9 years of criminal history, each offender was the subject of some 25 services or other correctional actions, at a median cost of $31,000 per program. The projected cost to the public by the time the 25 men were finally released from supervision in 1968, still at an early age, was calculated to total $10,000,000—that is $400,000 per man.

Correction officials operate in comparative isolation. They encounter the offender only after his conviction, by which time the person placed in their charge has already had a chance to become hardened, and they are provided very little opportunity for generating a positive motivation. At the end of the period

of institutionalization they see their charges returned to an outside world where they are met by hostility and very little opportunity for self-improvement.

Of more than 120,000 people employed in correctional institutions, only 20 per cent have any connection with rehabilitation. The balance are responsible for the custody and security
of the inmates. The work load for the 20 per cent assigned to
rehabilitation is obviously impossible: one teacher for every 150
inmates; one social worker for every 300 inmates; one counselor
for every 750 inmates; one psychiatrist for every 1,000 inmates;
one vocational guidance advisor for every 2,000 inmates.

The dehumanizing relationships among inmates is one aspect
of institutional life which is seldom discussed in polite society.
Sexual attacks are reported frequently. A recent investigation
of conditions in Philadelphia prisons found that there had been
approximately two thousand sexual assaults during a twenty-six-
month period, and that virtually every slightly built young man
committed to jail was approached within hours of his first admission and in many cases overwhelmed and raped by his fellow
inmates. Other repugnant aspects of prison life which appear to
be fairly commonplace include beatings, physical abuses, repeated indignities and, occasionally, violent deaths. *The New
York Times* reported in 1971 that there had been fifteen violent
deaths in the West Virginia State Penitentiary in the preceding
three years. Six inmates were slain, five committed suicide, three
were poisoned and one was burned to death. The local prosecuting attorney described the institution as "a monster machine
that turns out nothing but animals." A former state director of
corrections said that he had visited zoos that were cleaner and
safer than the state penitentiary. The traumatic impact of such
incidents on the personality and outlook of inmates who are
being prepared for return to decent society cannot be overstated.

EX-OFFENDERS

The man or woman who is convicted of a crime and processed through the correctional system does not stand much of

a chance in the outside world. Testifying before the New York City Commission on Human Rights in 1972, Harold Baer, Jr., former chief of the criminal division in the United States Attorney's Office, told the Commission that one of the most serious obstacles facing the ex-offender is the bar to employment:

> Employment is a sine qua non of rehabilitation for the majority of ex-offenders. If they cannot regain some element of self-respect, ex-offenders will almost inevitably return to crime.

The employment obstacles for former inmates involve both public attitudes and legal restrictions. The following list of legal handicaps imposed on persons convicted of a crime in New York State was compiled by a subcommittee of the National Association of Social Workers:

Right to Vote. Anyone convicted of a felony is prohibited from registering or voting in an election under the New York State election law.

Armed Forces. Convicted felons are excluded from military service.

Automobile Registration and License. The New York State Division of Motor Vehicles will not issue a registration certificate, operator's or chauffeur's license to a person who has been convicted of a felony without the approval of the parole officer or similar supervising personnel.

Hack License. Although no legal prohibition appears to exist, by standing rule licenses to drive taxicabs are automatically refused to persons convicted of felonies.

Public Housing. Standards employed by the New York City Housing Authority permit rejection of prospective tenants who have criminal records. On occasion, the Housing Authority has instituted eviction proceedings against the wife and children of a man who has been sentenced on a felony conviction.

Fishing Licenses. Permits for fishing in the New York City watershed area in upstate New York may be denied to persons with records of a felony conviction.

Civil Service. Persons with prison records stand little chance of being appointed to civil service positions, even though they may qualify through merit examination. Agency executives almost invariably select candidates who have no prior criminal record.

Employment. A felony conviction serves as an absolute or discretionary bar to employment in the following professions and licensed activities:

Architecture	Nursing
Billiard Halls	Optometry
Certain Union positions	Pharmacy
Certified Public Accountant	Podiatry
Check Cashing Agencies	Private Detectives
Chiropractice	Private Investigators
Dentistry	Professional Engineering
Embalming	Psychology
Insurance Adjustors	Real Estate Selling
Land Surveying	Shorthand Reporting
Landscape Architecture	Social Work
Masseuring	Undertaking
Medicine	Veterinary Medicine
Notaries Public	

A 1973 study by the American Bar Association unearthed almost 2,000 job licensing restrictions against ex-offenders in the 50 states and the District of Columbia, ranging from a high of 80 statutory provisions in Connecticut to a low of 21 in South Dakota.

The denial of employment opportunities to those who have criminal records is founded largely on superstition and ignorance. The unspoken premise is that a person who is convicted of a crime has a "criminal mind," and should be quarantined like a person with a communicable disease—people with "criminal minds" should not be allowed to infect respectable businesses, their employees or customers. A criminal record is a modern form of leprosy.

There is no secret voodoo or witchcraft casting a spell on some individuals to make them "criminals" and on others to make them "good citizens." There is, in fact, no such general classification as the "criminal mind." A small minority of persons convicted of crime have psychopathic personalities and are given to irrational, uncontrollable or dangerous conduct, but most of those we classify as "criminals" are ordinary people, with essentially the same basic personalities and characteristics as those who never see the inside of a courthouse. Extraneous circumstances usually make the difference—home environment, bad associations, desperation or simply temptation. All of us have a little larceny in our hearts. As Mark Twain once observed, "Every one is a moon, and has a dark side which he never shows to anybody." Any student of anthropology knows that the human personality, which has evolved over the course of 340,000 years and has only been "civilized" for a tiny fraction of that time, has its animal side, with all the accompanying weaknesses of anger, avarice and hatred. How can we conceivably justify the proposition that because a man has been convicted of a crime, he has a "criminal" personality and is irresistibly prone to vices unknown to the rest of us?

There is no logic to the view that a man who has committed a crime should not be permitted to move freely in law-abiding society, live freely among law-abiding neighbors or work freely among law-abiding fellow employees. It may be logical to determine in a specific case that there are factors present which may make one individual a poor risk in a particular line of work. But such a determination must be based on fact, not prejudice and superstition. A criminal record provides a proper basis only for inquiry and evaluation, not blind exclusion. Where the personality of an individual convicted of a crime is so potentially dangerous to the safety of his fellow citizens that he should not move about freely at all, then the sentencing judge and those who are responsible for institutional supervision and treatment should make sure that he is not turned loose until the personality disorder has been brought under control. But it is senseless to release a man convicted of crime back into society on the assumption that he will rehabilitate himself, and then deny him the fundamental opportunity for rehabilitation through a decent job.

The statutes prohibiting employment of persons with criminal records in certain lines of work are generally as unsound as they are unfair. The notion that a person with a felony conviction may not work as a dishwasher in a restaurant that serves alcoholic beverages is beyond comprehension. Such statutes usually are enacted by legislators on the basis of good intentions and colossal ignorance. Unfortunately, they often accurately reflect public attitudes. It is those public attitudes which need changing even more than the laws. What people must realize is that in a great many cases the effect of denying worthwhile jobs to people who have committed criminal violations in the past can well force them into a lifetime of further crime. The man or woman who is constantly reminded that he has no real chance to start a new and different life really has only one choice left—to go back to the old one.

Even more unjust is the job discrimination against those who have merely been arrested but never adjudicated guilty. Although anyone connected with law enforcement is well aware that the fact of arrest without conviction can never be treated as proof of guilt, most laymen take a different view. If a man has been arrested, they reason, he must have done something wrong and therefore should be quarantined.

A few years ago a bill was introduced in the New York State Legislature to prohibit employers from asking job applicants if they had ever been arrested ("arrested"—not "convicted"). The bill was killed in committee because of the intercession of lobbyists for public utilities, who claimed that they needed to find out about arrest records in order to protect customers against repairmen or meter readers who might have propensities to commit crime. While one can agree with the goal, blocking this bill was hardly the way to accomplish it. No one would quarrel with proper screening and personality tests for those who in fact go into people's homes, but an arrest record plays no necessary part of such screening. Meanwhile, all those job applicants who might be employed to work in the office, in the shop or in the field on operations which have no direct contact with the general public are penalized because of the narrow vision of the lobbyists. Much more important, job applicants for every other manner of employment in the state are also penalized. It is the height of injustice for two or three legislative representatives to be able to deny fair play to thousands of fellow citizens who deserve a chance to earn their own way into decent society through their own efforts and hard work.

Despite the overall gloomy outlook for the correction system in the United States, there are some bright spots. One of these has been the experience in California, where for the past ten years the prison system has been in the throes of a major overhaul, putting into practice many of the reforms that are still in the discussion stage in other parts of the country. The results so far have been extremely impressive. The high points include vocational training keyed to job opportunities, broad educational services, counseling and therapy, conjugal family visiting and an affirmative program for recruiting minority staff members. Prison populations are down in California, and so is recidivism. Prison officials still see many remaining problems. But at least they have begun the process of coping with them.

Another bright spot has been the recent passage in four states of laws providing that a person cannot be denied a license solely because of a criminal offense. These are important first steps on a long, long road.

Chapter 10

Let the Punishment
Fit the Crime—
and the Criminal

MUNICIPAL authorities in New York City recently declared war on youngsters armed with spray paint and felt-tipped markers. The hostilities followed a rash of grafitti-writing on subway cars and buses. The grafitti was an expression of youthful exuberance in the form of names and street numbers written in bright colors ("Pancho 123," "Louis 180," "Stud 141") rather than the more usual vulgarities. The authorities nonetheless branded the artists "vandals." The City Council was duly convened to deal with the problem. After weeks of deliberation and heated speechmaking, the Council finally enacted new "tough" legislation specifically aimed at grafitti writers. The ultimate remedy? Send the kids to prison for up to *three months*.

The City Council's response was typical of the heavy-handed, unimaginative approach to new social problems that has characterized most criminal statutes enacted in the last half-century. The standard approach of legislators is to make anything they cannot cope with a crime, and pass the problem over to the police, prosecutors and judges. But who is going to sentence a ten-year-old boy to prison for writing his name on a subway wall? What conceivable good would that do? Plainly the Council's objective was to discourage grafitti art by threatening severe punishment, but if the threat is hollow, it accomplishes nothing;

and if—God forbid—it were ever carried out, the result would be the start of a career in law-breaking, beginning with the liberal education provided by fellow inmates in any of our inadequate penal institutions.

Prison sentences are not the general cure-all for anti-social conduct. Because of our substantial ignorance of how to control human behavior, imprisonment may be our only tool in a narrow group of special cases, but our present wholesale reliance on it is both cruel and counterproductive.

Our approach to sentencing and correction suffers from the same schizophrenia affecting our attitude toward antisocial conduct in general. On the one hand we seek to deter potential violators from committing some offense. On the other, we seek to rehabilitate the individual who has violated the law so that we can ensure his good conduct for the future. The difficulty is that the two objectives are distinctly different, and cannot be combined effectively. A man who is being punished is not likely to be receptive to rehabilitation, which requires a sense of motivation and hope for the future. The type of facilities that are used to deprive a man of his liberty are generally not suitable for rehabilitating him. We would make much more progress if we were to separate out the two objectives and deal with them independently.

PROPER USES OF IMPRISONMENT

In theory, the purpose of enacting statutes that authorize long prison sentences is to discourage people from violating the law. But the function of deterrence breaks down when sentences are not imposed as contemplated by the law, or where violators are not apprehended or prosecuted promptly. Take, for example, the offense of bribery. Because many businessmen put profits above ethics, the payment of bribes is rarely reported and therefore infrequently prosecuted. Moreover, even when prosecution does take place, the attitudes reflected by sentencing judges have little deterrent effect at all.

Under Federal law, bribery of a public employee is punishable by imprisonment of up to fifteen years and a fine of ten thousand dollars. Yet in case after case of admitted bribery of Internal Revenue Service agents by attorneys and accountants, the fines generally meted out constitute a mere fraction of the amount of income which the offender was attempting to conceal. In the rare case where a prison sentence is imposed, the length of sentence is comparatively short. In one recent case, a certified public accountant who pleaded guilty to having paid an IRS agent a ten-thousand-dollar bribe received a fine of only one thousand dollars and was placed on probation. An attorney pleading guilty to having paid a thousand-dollar bribe in a matter concerning a client's tax deficiency of thirty thousand dollars was placed on probation for one year and fined two thousand dollars. In another case, involving commercial bribery, the Federal judge who suspended sentence expressly stated that one of his reasons was that the offense was commonplace in the business community. The substantial likelihood that a defendant will not be punished severely if caught destroys the deterrent effect of the penalties provided by statute. Of course imprisonment is not the only sanction that might discourage potential offenders from violating the law, but if we intend it to serve such a purpose then statutory penalties should be reviewed with this goal in mind and rewritten to ensure that adequate sentences are imposed for serious offenses in all cases to deter other would-be violators.

Wholly apart from the question of deterrence, there are at least two other valid grounds for the use of imprisonment. The first is to separate antisocial individuals from the rest of society so that they cannot harm others. Obviously this is a concession that our rehabilitation procedures have failed, but it would be foolhardy to pretend that we know how to direct every malefactor back onto the road of good conduct. There are many persons who simply cannot be reached by our present limited techniques and resources, and in these cases the only available procedure to protect society from harm is sequestration. Specifically, defendants with the demonstrated uncontrollable disposition to commit serious crimes of violence against innocent people must be removed from society until their potential for harm has been eliminated or minimized.

The second legitimate social basis for imposing prison sentences is to utilize sanctions creatively in compelling convicted criminals to make amends for their injury to society. This can usually be accomplished through their cooperation with law enforcement officials in providing evidence concerning crimes committed by associates and others. A narcotics offender, for example, often will not betray his source of heroin supply unless he is facing the possibility of a substantial prison term. The courts can help to break up large narcotics smuggling rings by imposing such a term and encouraging the lower-level operatives to testify against their superiors in return for the hope of a reduced prison sentence.

The prison facility itself deserves more careful consideration in cases where the purpose of imprisonment is deterrence, seclusion or cooperation, rather than rehabilitation. Such an institution should be primarily custodial in nature, and should provide the prisoner with a decent if spartan existence, administered humanely and in keeping with the standards of civilized society. The essential object must be confinement, not the imposition of special indignities, cruelty or abuse. If the concept of imprisonment has any validity as a deterrent force, then it should be limited simply to the deprivation of liberty for a particular segment of the offender's lifetime, and should not involve punishments meant to be actually destructive, such as solitary confinement.

PRETRIAL DIVERSION

One of the most dramatic insights achieved in recent years has been the realization that many offenders become hardened criminals during the course of receiving "due process" in our criminal justice system. Many factors contribute to this: contact in detention facilities with older violators; exposure to lawyers who look upon justice as a game one wins or loses; firsthand experience with the injustices of disparate sentencing practices, or differences in the quality of legal representation depending on one's financial resources; education by "jailhouse lawyers" in how legal procedures can be manipulated to win delays; plus the desire to find a scapegoat and, if possible, a loophole to beat the charge. All these factors contribute to a personality development and outlook totally at odds with the notion of accommodating to society and building a new life. By the time a defendant has been turned over to correction officials under the standard arrest-arraignment-motions-trial-sentence-appeal approach to criminal justice, the chances for his successful rehabilitation have faded considerably.

Against this background, the most promising new approach to rehabilitation has been a procedure called "pretrial diversion." Pretrial diversion means placing a defendant in a rehabilitation program—with his consent—immediately after arrest, the prosecutor having agreed to drop all charges if the rehabilitation program is successful. To date, this concept has depended primarily on enlightened prosecutors. Professional rehabilitation personnel, trained to diagnose offender personalities and plan rehabilitation programs, have customarily been relegated to the postconviction period and not allowed to contribute their skills during this important phase. But the success of the pretrial diversion approach indicates that there is need for extensive commitment of professional manpower to diagnose and classify offenders immediately after arrest, instead of waiting until after the trial and adjudication process. The important thing is to be able to start the rehabilitation process as soon as possible after the offender has been taken into custody. This is the ideal psychological moment for developing strong motivation for change, since many offenders are acutely aware of their guilt immediately after apprehension and are anxious to make amends and turn to a different life.

Of course pretrial diversion does not fit every case or every individual, but its high success rate does demonstrate that the entire rehabilitation phase of the criminal justice system should be integrated into the process from the moment of arrest to the moment of final release. This means that the professionals who know how to analyze personality problems and prescribe treatment and training programs (which should include ex-offenders and others who can relate to the subject's background, and not just products of social work schools) should participate from the very beginning. It also means that personality diagnosis should be just as routine a postarrest procedure as the taking of fingerprints. Most probation officers are hesitant to discuss anything about a defendant's background while criminal charges are pending, yet this attitude makes no sense at all if the defendant himself is willing to open up his problems for discussion.

By attempting an immediate diagnosis and classification following arrest, experienced professionals can then make recommendations concerning the optimum future handling of the offender. Presumably this would involve one of the following options:

Pretrial diversion and community supervision for those offenders who would be responsive to this approach.

Institutional treatment for special problems such as alcoholism, narcotics addiction or personality disorders; or confinement to a specialized institutional setting which might provide better supportive services (such institutionalization to be either by consent, civil commitment or subsequent to conviction).

Detention and immediate trial for offenders who have personality profiles which pose genuine dangers to society, to be followed by institutional sequestration until the condition has been corrected or tempered by time.

Or no rehabilitation or treatment indicated.

Obviously these approaches cannot work without the adoption of an entirely new ethic by lawyers who represent defendants in criminal proceedings. The sporting theory of justice must be abandoned (except, of course, in cases where a defendant maintains his innocence). The defense attorney must begin to concentrate on the long-range best interests of his client, rather than just trying to win some temporary advantage through a tactical maneuver or loophole.

USE OF CIVIL REMEDIES

The courts have been swamped with new types of criminal offenses and new variations on old offenses primarily because of the lack of creativity by Congress and the state legislatures in finding more workable remedies. For anyone schooled in the law, the most obvious oversight in these statutes has been the failure to utilize the wide range of flexible techniques available on the civil side of the courts. The largely untapped civil jurisdiction offers effective sanctions for the handling of many antisocial acts with which our present criminal law has been unable to cope. Comparing the criminal justice system with the available civil alternatives in terms of their deterrence potential and ability to compensate the victims of crime is a revelation in itself. How frequently we convict someone who has preyed on large numbers of innocent victims and then do nothing to help his victims, much less deter others from following his course.

The immediate benefits from using the civil side of the court to deal with antisocial conduct are apparent. Civil proceedings mean full discovery by both sides. Such proceedings permit action through motions for preliminary injunctions and summary judgment. They also mean that the prosecutor need only prove his case by a preponderance of evidence, not beyond a reasonable doubt. Where equitable remedies are sought, the time-consuming jury process is unnecessary. The use of special masters and magistrates to supervise fact-finding hearings can expand the capability of the court to handle a high turnover. If the civil side can provide a more effective remedy, therefore, while using more simplified proceedings, the benefits to all concerned is readily apparent. (One must candidly recognize that the delay in civil cases can be even worse than in criminal cases, but this need not be so—an Order to Show Cause is a fast-moving writ in the right hands.)

Plainly we should not substitute one set of rigid remedies for another, but we do need a much more flexible approach in dealing with antisocial conduct, with a full range of remedies available to the trial judge for application as circumstances warrant. At the present time, the trial judge's options are extremely limited. Essentially there are three:

Imposition of a suspended sentence and possible placement of the defendant on probation for a period of supervision by a caseworker.

Imprisonment.

Imposition of a fine, within fixed statutory limits.

Many trial judges who recognize the futility of just locking up a defendant for a long time nevertheless feel frustrated by these limitations, particularly when they see defendants going through the revolving door of the law to commit crimes again, or when they hear critics charge that the courts are too lenient. These are some additional remedies that might be provided by utilizing the civil side of the court:

Judicial Censure

Approximately 56 per cent of all sentences imposed by the Federal courts in the fiscal year ending June 30, 1971, involved no prison sentences whatsoever. In most of these cases, the only result of the prosecution was a criminal record for the defendant. Why should the entire criminal court machinery be utilized if a judicial record of wrongdoing will be the only predictable result? The judicial censure is a familiar sanction used against lawyers who are found guilty of professional misconduct but who are not going to be suspended or disbarred. Why not utilize this same remedy for private citizens and even public officials guilty of certain classes of misconduct? For the attorney in disciplinary proceedings, the matter is handled on the civil side of the court. There is no reason why a similar procedure should not be used where the anticipated remedy includes a public adjudication of misconduct. Realistically, the fear of public exposure and shame because of attendant publicity is one of the most significant factors involved in criminal prosecutions of businessmen and public officials. The same thing could be accomplished on the civil side, with simpler procedures and speedier results.

Monetary Penalty

The criminal law already recognizes the value of fines as a judicial sanction, realizing that economic loss can be very strong punishment in the proper circumstances. The problem is that for many defendants, particularly in white-collar cases, the maximum limits are ludicrously small. For example, the present maximum fine for mail fraud is one thousand dollars. Why do we not expand the fine concept through a civil penalty procedure, which would include a full inquiry into the violator's economic resources as a way of determining the most meaningful type of monetary penalty? The maximum penalty, say, might be 50 per cent of a man's entire net worth. A five-thousand-dollar fine may be insignificant to a millionaire, whereas to a blue-collar worker with a mortgage on his home it could be devastating. Such a fixed penalty obviously is no deterrent for a man who can accumulate vast wealth from his illegal operations. He would consider it merely a cost of doing business, and a small one at that.

Injunction

The greatest weapon in the legal arsenal is the injunction. The equitable injunction can make people do things that should be done, and stop them from doing things that should not be done. Backing up the injunction is an imposing contempt power, strong enough to insure compliance by virtually anyone.

The injunction can achieve miracles in forcing compliance with the law in situations where a criminal conviction would have almost no impact. Recently, criminal proceedings were brought against a mail-order firm which had shipped untaxed cigarettes into New York State in huge quantities, resulting in the loss to the state of thousands of dollars in tax revenues. Following conviction, after an extended period of delay, the defendant was fined the sum of one thousand dollars, a fraction of the total amount of taxes that had been evaded. Almost the very next day, the owner of the business started operations again under a new corporate name. As a countermove, the United States Attorney's Office then turned to the civil side of the court and in a matter of days succeeded in obtaining injunctions against the new firm plus a large group of other major cigarette-mailing companies and their individual owners, barring them from using the mails without complying with all local tax requirements. The effect of this approach proved far superior to any that might have been gained by another criminal prosecution, for within a short time, illegal mailings of untaxed cigarettes into New York came to a virtual standstill.

Civil injunctive relief has also proven itself more effective than criminal punishment in enforcing antipollution laws. In a recent case, the Federal government successfully obtained a civil injunction under which the defendant was required to clean up not only its local plant, but also every other plant it owned throughout the country, at a total cost of nearly $45,000,000. If the Government had proceeded criminally, the maximum possible fine would have been $250,000.

Restitution and Damages

Many perpetrators of securities fraud, forgery, smuggling, larceny and similar offenses involving multiple transactions with large numbers of investors or purchasers can profit handsomely from their illegal activities despite the possibility of criminal prosecution. This is because their victims are usually without resources to seek restitution or damages, and the available sanctions for the criminal violation do not include repayment of money stolen or obtained by fraud. How much more significant it would be to have the court require the defendant to pay over all illegal profits for the benefit of the victims, who might then be reimbursed upon filing a simple verified proof of claim. Even more effective as a deterrent would be authorization for law enforcement officers to seek double or treble damages for the benefit of the victims.

Treatment

A number of crimes are committed by people who suffer from some form of personality disorder. Through early screening and prompt referral, many defendants arrested for criminal conduct can be put on the road to recovery through supervision and guidance. For some defendants, psychiatric care can achieve good results, sometimes through attendance at clinics, sometimes through institutionalized treatment. Specific conditions which contribute to antisocial conduct, such as narcotics addiction, can often be corrected by prompt and proper help. Civil commitment for purposes of receiving care when indicated should be more widely employed as an alternative to the ritual criminal procedure of trial, sentence and appeal. Providing long-term supervision and follow-up would be a major improvement over present procedures which permit an institution to discharge a disturbed personality whenever it chooses.

Providing alternative civil sanctions can be achieved quite simply—by enacting into law a single statute authorizing the use of a range of civil sanctions in a specifically identified group of offenses. Under the statute, the civil sanctions could be available either *in addition to,* or *as alternatives to,* existing criminal sanctions. The initial choice as to whether criminal or civil sanctions would be sought would then rest with the prosecutor, just as prosecutors presently decide whether or not to institute a criminal prosecution. If the prosecutor initiates the case as a criminal action, and the defendant is convicted, then the court itself would have the further option of imposing either criminal sanctions or civil sanctions, or a *combination* of the two. In the reverse situation, however, in which the prosecutor instituted the proceedings on the civil side, the court would be limited only to civil sanctions and would not be able to impose criminal ones.

Where the action is instituted as a criminal case, then all the full due process guarantees of the Constitution and rules of criminal procedure would apply, from grand jury indictment through appellate remedies. Where the action is instituted as a civil case, the civil rules of procedure would apply, including full mutual discovery rights. Obviously rules as to the burden of proof would also shift depending on the nature of the proceeding.

This stroke-of-the-pen change in the array of remedies available to public prosecutors would bring about a dramatic revolution in their work. Many local prosecutors do not now even have the power to exercise civil jurisdiction. They must bring cases on the criminal side or not at all. In marked contrast is the Federal concept, which combines both criminal and civil powers in the United States Attorneys in each district.

The following breakdown is offered for discussion purposes as a basis for the allocation of remedies:

Category I.   Criminal Sanctions Only

The types of offenses for which prison sentences seem most clearly appropriate, either to protect society, generate cooperation in undoing the harm that has been done, or deter other would-be offenders, are those involving extreme violence, organized crime activities and narcotics trafficking. For these few cases, because of their seriousness, the legislature might well conclude that neither prosecutor nor judge should have the option to employ civil remedies. Indeed, a strong case could be made for providing a mandatory minimum sentence.

Category II.   Criminal and/or Civil Sanctions

The bulk of the present group of statutory crimes could well be reclassified to give the prosecutor the option of deciding whether to proceed on the criminal or civil side of the court, and to give the court the option of determining whether criminal or civil sanctions should actually be imposed. These crimes include various types of fraud, larceny, corruption and related offenses.

Category III.   *Civil Sanctions Only*

A third grouping of lesser offenses should be removed from the criminal courts entirely. These are the so-called victimless crimes: gambling, prostitution, narcotics use, drunkenness, disorderly conduct and the like.

The flexible approach suggested here would reduce the number of hard-core criminal cases that could be handled only in the criminal courts to about 3 per cent of the present total. Those that would be subject to criminal and/or civil sanctions would constitute 25 per cent of the total. The remaining 72 per cent would be civil or administrative cases only. What this would mean in terms of reducing the burden on our criminal courts is self-evident. But what it could mean in terms of more meaningful and effective enforcement of the law might be truly revolutionary.

Chapter 11

The Individual, Government and the Courts

CORA WALKER is black. She also is a lawyer, the mother of two sons, active in Harlem community affairs and a woman with a strong sense of right and wrong. The day she graduated from high school she took over responsibility of the support of her family, which until then had depended on public welfare. Cora Walker worked at night while she put herself through college and law school. After years of struggle as a young lawyer, she had saved enough to open her own law office. She bought a four-story brownstone on Lenox Avenue, in the heart of Harlem, and completely renovated it from cellar to roof, with her law office on the ground floor and residential units above. When she took over the building it was in terrible condition, like so many other tenements in the area. Toilets did not work, there was no hot water, the furnace was broken, the areaway was filled with rotting garbage. Floors, stairs, walls were in a state of decay. Ironically, as it turned out later, there were no municipal housing-code violations filed against the building.

Mrs. Walker invested a total of thirty thousand dollars in a complete renovation of the building—installing new wiring, new brass plumbing, new toilet fixtures, refrigerators, furnace, doors and lighting. Rats and roaches were driven out and the building placed in first-class condition. Then Mrs. Walker came face to face with something she had not expected.

Uneducated to the ways of municipal government in housing enforcement, Mrs. Walker naïvely applied for a Certificate of Occupancy, the final administrative approval of renovation that certifies legal use of a building. She encountered a series of stalling maneuvers: lost files, buck-passing, harassing inspections. Then someone took her aside and explained how the department "worked"—a bribe had to be paid. In the process of her accelerated education Mrs. Walker learned that the contractors had already paid $280 to three different building department inspectors for the privilege of being permitted to continue their work uninterrupted. Cora Walker did what she believed every good citizen should do: she went directly to the District Attorney and reported the whole incident. Detective Carl Bogan was assigned to the case, and he confirmed the fact that a fifty-dollar bribe had been solicited by a go-between for the inspectors. Somehow the inspectors had got wind of the investigation, however, and the payoff meeting never took place. Instead, Mrs. Walker began to be seesawed between the Department of Buildings and the Housing Court as technical violations piled up, one on top of another. When she blurted out in open court that the violations were part of a pattern to force her to pay a bribe, the roof fell in on her. Teams of inspectors swarmed all over her building. A new list of "violations" was written up, and now reprisals started in earnest.

While extreme housing decay went unnoticed and neglected in other tenement buildings, the full might of the Buildings Department was leveled against one solitary black woman who dared to fight the system. She was hauled into Housing Court and offered an opportunity to plead guilty in the name of a corporation, but she insisted instead on standing trial. She was convicted on a record in which trial judge Manuel Gomez brazenly blocked every effort by the defendant to introduce evidence of the circumstances which had prompted the unfair prosecution. The conviction was appealed to the State's highest court, and there reversed with direction to the trial court to

hear evidence on Mrs. Walker's claim that she had been uncon-
stitutionally selected for harassment because of her refusal to
pay a bribe. More proceedings followed, extending over three
and a half years, but finally Cora Walker was vindicated. The
Appellant Term of the Supreme Court of the State of New York
handed down a decision unanimously reversing her conviction
for housing-code violations. The court held that Mrs. Walker
had demonstrated by a clear preponderance of evidence that
she had been singled out for criminal prosecution by an inten-
tional, purposeful and unusual selection process, which was in
sharp contrast to the existing pattern of enforcement of housing
laws in New York City, and that the time allowed her to correct
the alleged violations was so unreasonably short as to make
correction an impossibility and criminal conviction a certainty.
The court declared:

> The evidence leads irresistibly to the conclusion that this in-
> tentional discrimination and prosecution was in retaliation
> for defendant's public exposure of corruption in the Depart-
> ment of Buildings and was in no wise aimed at securing com-
> pliance with the housing laws. In view of the prior proceed-
> ings herein, the evidence adduced by defendant at the pretrial
> hearing below required dismissal of the prosecution on the
> ground that defendant was deprived of her constitutional right
> to equal protection of laws.

Cora Walker, believe it or not, was lucky. She knew her
rights and she had a lawyer to represent her in court. The sad
fact is that most of her neighbors do not have the same advantage. Ignorance of legal rights and the unavailability of professional or other assistance in dealing with administrative
agencies or the courts is one of the most serious problems facing
people of low and moderate income in American society. The
National Commission on the Causes and Prevention of Violence
pointed to this deficiency as one of the important elements in
the pattern of lawlessness and violence which erupted in the
United States during the 1960's, in large measure generated
by frustration and protest against a system which appeared
heartless and unconcerned with the needs of the individual. A

staff report for the Commission noted that special government agencies established to help the poor often had created a brand new set of legal problems and spawned new sources of frustration. Instead of improving matters, these administrative agencies and government services had in many cases made them worse.

Welfare was cited as an example of a governmental administrative function which adds to fear and confusion among its intended beneficiaries. The staff report pointed out that welfare intrudes into every aspect of recipients' lives, determining where they live and with whom, whether their children get new clothes for school, what kind of food they buy and at which store they buy it, and where they go when they are sick. Commented the report: "It is like lifelong probation." Eligibility for welfare presents one set of problems. Continuation on the welfare rolls presents another. Regulations are complex and comprehensive. In Los Angeles, the regulations governing welfare administration actually weigh 115 pounds. Sudden cutbacks in benefits at the whim of the legislature or in spurts of governmental economizing make the individual beneficiary's life precarious.

Public housing is another governmental function which can be heartless and bureaucratic in its administration. Because the number of dwelling units is far short of the demand in most cities, waiting lists are long and housing administrations can exercise almost dictatorial powers in determining who will be chosen. Political influence frequently plays an important role in these determinations, and uneducated housing applicants who do not know how to contact their elected representatives for assistance are at a great disadvantage.

Many other government programs designed to help the poor can become a torment to them instead, including public education, housing-code inspections, health services, consumer-fraud bureaus, civil rights commissions, and other well-intentioned but poorly managed public bodies. Frequently the failure of the appropriate governmental agencies to function properly is directly related to the inability of the uneducated poor to lodge complaints which will receive attention. Most public agencies depend on complaints to trigger their services, and when the complaints do not materialize the programs do not move. Further weakening their ability to function are the problems of insufficient manpower, low salaries and high staff turnover. Political opportunists regularly expose "scandals" in poverty-oriented agencies, demoralizing the staff and frequently triggering budget cuts. It is no wonder, then, that staff members themelves try to avoid rocking the boat and tend to take a compromising view of any wrong involving one of the agency's clients. Exposés usually generate new administrative controls, which mean more paper work, more reports and more studies by agency employees, and less time left for them to concentrate on serving their intended beneficiaries. The urban poor thus begin to distrust government and politicians and do not think affirmatively in terms of utilizing governmental aid to help them with personal problems.

The outlook for persons above the poverty level, in the moderate-income bracket, is not much better. In fact, for many it is worse. Since they cannot qualify for poverty-type assistance they have to use their own resources to obtain help. When it comes to lawyers this is virtually impossible, because fee structures are not geared to persons of moderate income, and attorneys employed by legal aid societies and poverty agencies are not permitted to work for people above certain income levels.

People of moderate means have a jaundiced view of government. They see a proliferation of programs to aid the poor, but not many agencies available to help those above the poverty line. Although wooed at election time, most people of moderate income regard themselves as disenfranchised. In a recent survey of public attitudes, 49 per cent of those with incomes of $5,000 a year felt that they had no say about what the government does; in the income bracket between $5,000 and $9,999, the figure was 33 per cent; while among persons with incomes of over $10,000 it shrank to 26 per cent. Similarly, 57 per cent of people with annual incomes of $5,000 felt that public officials do not care what they think. For those in the $5,000 to $9,999 bracket, the figure was 42 per cent, and for those with incomes of $10,000 and over, it was 31 per cent. Educational levels produced the same pattern: 49 per cent of those with eighth-grade educations felt that they had no say in government, 33 per cent of the high school graduates felt that way, while only 2 per cent of the college graduates shared that view.

When government was simpler and cities were less complex, the local political leader often performed the role of special friend and advisor for people of low and moderate means, and the neighborhood political club served as a clearinghouse for problems involving government or the courts. But times have changed. The political clubhouse has largely disappeared as a social-service institution, and the local elected representative has increasingly taken on the chore of representing constituents with governmental needs. Many legislators, however, particularly those in the minority party of the legislative body in which they serve, have inadequate staff to deal with any substantial number of individual problems. Citizens who do manage to get attention and help from their elected representatives therefore receive an advantage out of proportion to those who do not. Generally speaking, a letter from a state legislator or a congressman puts a chill in the heart of any administrator, who would much rather comply with the legislator's request than run the risk of being criticized on the floor of the legislature, or jeopardizing his agency's budget. People who can have letters written on their behalf by legislators, therefore, usually get exceptionally good service. The problem is that most people do not get this kind of attention.

THE OMBUDSMAN IDEA

Several years ago there was a wide interest in the possibility of importing the European institution of the "Ombudsman," an official trouble-shooter for citizens with complaints involving government agencies. Professor Walter Gellhorn of Columbia Law School prepared two significant texts on the subject and testified before a string of legislative committees, relating the successful experiences of Denmark, Finland, New Zealand, Norway, Sweden, Yugoslavia, Poland, the Soviet Union and Japan. In 1967, the American Assembly, made up of representatives of business, education, communications, labor, government and the professions, recommended the adoption of the ombudsman concept in state and local governments. Pointing out that millions of Americans view government as distant and unresponsive, if not hostile, the American Assembly urged that the means by which individual citizens can voice dissatisfaction with governmental action or inaction should be improved in order to make society more democratically effective. As envisioned in its recommendation, the ombudsman would serve as an independent, high-level officer to receive complaints, pursue inquiries and make recommendations for appropriate action. He would have the power to initiate his own investigations and to make public reports when appropriate. His principal weapons would be persuasion, criticism and publicity. He would not have direct legal power to change administrative action or rulings. The usual procedure upon receipt of complaint would be for the ombudsman to ask the agency involved for an explanation, this to be followed by further consultations with the complainant and the agency until the matter was satisfactorily resolved. The ideal ombudsman would be selected in a manner to insure full public confidence in his independence, impartiality and professional ability. He would receive a good salary and have the power to select his own staff, and his term of office would not be dependent upon the chief executive of the governmental unit in which he worked. The authority of the ombudsman would extend to all public agencies except the courts, legislature and chief executive.

Despite these recommendations and an apparently widespread interest in the idea, the concept of the ombudsman never did catch hold in America in any meaningful way. Here and there an experimental program was started, but little of significance has been achieved. In 1971, Mayor Kenneth Gibson announced that Newark, New Jersey, had received the nation's first Federal grant for the establishment of an ombudsman to investigate city agencies. The total budget for the experiment was $150,000. Little other interest has been shown.

Undoubtedly one of the reasons the ombudsman idea has not proven popular with legislators, who must provide the necessary authority and funds, is that such an office would be competitive with services which they themselves render to their constituents as a way of building up goodwill for election day. Another likely reason is resistance from administrative agencies, many of which already have complaint procedures and most of whom quite naturally do not want to encourage any more "trouble" than is necessary. The extent and effectiveness of existing complaint machinery is, however, spotty at best. In 1969, the Civil Rights Committee of the New York County Lawyers Association conducted a survey on the handling of citizen complaints by administrative agencies in the New York metropolitan area. The study produced discouraging results. Common citizen complaints covered such topics as street cleaning, garbage and snow removal, dishonest or unfair employees, poor behavior, bad service, bureaucracy and red tape, welfare, taxes, need for more facilities, fire violations, rudeness, lack of justice, discrimination, consumer protection, housing, bad laws and regulations, delays in receiving benefits, poor advice and wrong advice. Agencies varied widely in their accessibility to complainants. In some agencies complaints were handled with courtesy, in others the complainant was required to file a statement in writing. Knowledgeable employees handled complaints in some agencies, uninterested clerks handled them in others. Internal breakdowns within agencies in forwarding problems to those who could do something about them was commonplace. In many agencies no record at all was kept of complaints, and they could be easily misplaced and neglected. Procedures for recording and processing them varied widely, as did efficiency and courtesy. The Committee noted that mutual protectiveness among employees frequently prevented proper consideration of complaints addressed to agency procedures which might be regarded as critical of their work. Overall, the impression gained of complaint procedures was disheartening. Though most agencies surveyed insisted that they were doing an excellent job, careful scrutiny indicated just the contrary. Too often the citizen was given the wrong person to speak to, or directed to the wrong agency altogether.

THE INDIVIDUAL IN THE COURTS

The plight of the individual of low or moderate means within the court system is equally disheartening. Private litigants in the lower courts often number in the tens of thousands each year and are processed through the court system as little more than statistics. Specialized courts have been created to handle many of their problems, such as those dealing with the family, juveniles, landlord-tenant relations and small claims. In most of these minor courts the defendant has virtually no access to legal assistance and is on his own, even though he may be confronted with problems of evidence and other legal questions which he cannot possibly anticipate or handle without some legal guidance. Courts dealing with social problems tend to rely primarily on probation officers or other social workers to identify the individual difficulty, but these personnel are themselves usually overworked and unable to give personal attention to the real needs of those they are meant to help.

The small-claims court is a particularly troublesome forum for legal redress. The original intent was a good one—to provide a court that would help the poor man collect his claim without unnecessary formalities or expense. Ironically, the small-claims court has been transformed primarily into a collection agency for department stores and other commercial claimants who can group large numbers of claims *against* poor people and process them quickly at little expense. A recent study of the small-claims court in Oakland, California, showed that two out of every three litigants were finance companies, mail-order houses, stores or local government agencies. Individual defendants were pitted against experienced claimants' attorneys in an atmosphere that pressured them toward settlement or pretty well assured that they would be overwhelmed if they insisted on a trial.

It would be unfair to conclude that the judges and referees who work in the small-claims courts are not considerate of the needs of those they are supposed to serve. But consideration is not enough. Even where a poor claimant is successful in obtaining a judgment, enforcement is nearly impossible because the amount of the claim usually does not justify the necessary fees for the marshal. Even though the court costs are greatly reduced, it is still ironic that individuals of limited income should be required to pay for the cost of operating the courts. The filing of fees, and other court expenses, can mount up to several dollars or more, and if the case is at all complicated the expenses for witnesses, transcripts or other court-related work can be quite substantial. In a day when most government agencies are financed out of tax monies and serve the public without charge, there seems little justification for penalizing individuals who seek redress in the courts by making them pay-as-they-go.

The ABA Code of Professional Responsibility says that lawyers have an obligation to provide legal services to those unable to pay for them: "Every lawyer, regardless of professional prominence or professional workload, should find time to participate in serving the disadvantaged." The traditional form for providing legal services to the disadvantaged has been through local Legal Aid societies. The New York City Legal Aid Society, for example, rendered legal assistance to 261,484 persons in 1971. The bulk of these cases are in the criminal courts, where the Society's record of dismissals and acquittals is more than creditable. But a substantial part of the Society's work involves direct assistance in civil matters such as family problems, landlord-tenant relations, contract claims, social benefits, job and license problems, torts, estate and property matters, immigration difficulties and other legal needs.

The basic deficiency in organized legal assistance programs for the poor, however, is that they are limited to people below a certain income level, leaving large numbers of persons of limited means without access to professional help. The standard of eligibility for a person to qualify for legal aid in New York is a maximum income of eighty-five dollars a week for a single person, or one hundred dollars a week for someone who is married. Under OEO legal services programs, the maximum income an individual may earn and still apply for free services is four thousand dollars per year plus four hundred dollars for each dependent. A recent Department of Commerce report indicates that 63 per cent of the nation's population earns between six thousand and fifteen thousand dollars per year. These are the people for whom legal services are not available in any real sense. The New York Legal Aid Society alone turns away five to six thousand people a year who are above its income limits. In the Civil Court of the City of New York, more than six thousand individuals of moderate means are forced to defend themselves without legal counsel in civil actions. It is estimated that fifty thousand people per year appear in the small-claims court in New York City without legal representation, and another fifty thousand must defend against landlord claims without attorneys.

One attempt to provide legal services for persons of moderate means has been the establishment of bar association lawyer-referral services. Usually such programs include a guaranteed initial consultation of half an hour for a fixed fee which is quite moderate, but thereafter the attorney is permitted to charge whatever fee the client is willing to pay. This approach, however, has had only limited impact on the total problem.

Increasing interest is being shown in the idea of prepaid legal services, similar to hospital and health insurance plans, and some successful experiments have been carried out with this type of legal representation, sometimes referred to as "Judicare." One of the first was organized in Shreveport, Louisiana, in co-operation with a major labor union located in the community. All 250 lawyers in Shreveport agreed to participate in the program. With a contribution of two cents per hour of his wages to the Shreveport Legal Services Corporation each union member became eligible for the following maximum benefits: $100 worth of consultive services, not to exceed $25 per visit; $250 for office work, including negotiations, research and investigations; $325 for legal fees; $40 for court costs; and $150 for out of pocket expenses in any judicial or administrative proceeding, plus 80 per cent of the next $1,000 in litigation expenses. (Office work benefits require an additional payment of $10 and judicial proceedings require a prepayment of $25.)

Another variant of prepaid legal services is a plan worked out between the Los Angeles County Bar Association and the California Teachers Association. Unlike the Shreveport plan, under which each client may choose any lawyer he wants, the Los Angeles plan requires selection from a panel of lawyers. Several insurance companies are now exploring the possibility of developing commercial insurance plans to provide the same type of services to persons who are not members of groups which can negotiate their own special programs. Not everyone is enthusiastic about the Judicare concept, though. A number of persons associated with poverty-law programs are critical of the voluntary participation that is part of the Judicare concept and regard it as far less efficient and more expensive than the use of salaried staff attorneys.

Even more troublesome than providing persons of limited means with lawyers is getting them to make use of their services. A recent American Bar Foundation survey of low-income families residing in a black ghetto in the Midwest disclosed that most were unaware of their rights and available remedies. The study concluded that, along with the expansion of free legal services, broad legal education programs are also needed to inform people of their rights and of the community resources which can provide help when these rights are threatened.

What all of this means is that much more attention must be paid to the fairness and adequacy of administrative and lower court procedures designed to serve persons of limited income. Above all, a literal explosion of legal services must be made available. Perhaps we have reached the point where we should adopt the French system of permitting laymen to render certain forms of legal advice and assistance. Certainly our present legal resources alone can never do the job.

Chapter 12

Youngsters in Trouble

AT the age of twenty-four, Lee Harvey Oswald gained the dubious distinction of becoming the most widely known political assassin in history. It was for him the climax of a series of episodes which parallelled the pattern of inadequate home life and upbringing of most youths who get into trouble with the law. Oswald's father died shortly before he was born. His mother, Marguerite, was forced to go to work to try to feed her three sons. Then, faced with utter poverty, she placed her two older children, John, aged seven, and Robert, five, in an orphans' home. When he reached the age of three, Lee Oswald was also sent to the home.

The following year, Marguerite Oswald withdrew her three offspring from the orphanage in anticipation of her marriage to another man. The marriage, however, did not last. Family relations were stormy and Oswald's mother divorced her second husband after three years. Mrs. Oswald complained bitterly of unfair treatment, and told her children that she now could not send them to a military academy, as she had hoped to do. Instead, she asked the oldest boy to quit school to help support the family. Money problems constantly plagued Marguerite Oswald. Her youngest son, Lee, would return after classes to an empty house while she was at work in an insurance business.

Lee Oswald did not play with other children his own age, and became increasingly withdrawn.

Shortly before his thirteenth birthday, Lee Harvey Oswald and his mother moved to New York City, where they lived briefly with Marguerite's eldest son, John, and his wife, while John was stationed there with the Coast Guard. During the course of an argument at the New York apartment, Oswald threatened his sister-in-law with a pocket knife and she reported the incident to her husband when he returned from work. Lee and his mother were asked to leave. Thereafter the boy enrolled in P.S. 117, a junior high school in the Bronx, where he was teased by other youngsters for his Texas accent and "Western" clothes. His interest in school diminished, and increasingly he stayed at home, reading magazines and watching television. Finally truancy charges were brought against him and he was remanded to Youth House, a juvenile detention facility, for psychiatric observation. The examining doctor found Lee Oswald tense, withdrawn and evasive. He disliked talking about himself and his feelings, and tried to give the impression that he did not care for other people. The doctor noted "intense anxiety, shyness, feelings of awkwardness and insecurity." The boy was described as having a "vivid fantasy life, turning around the topics of omnipotence and power, through which he tries to compensate for his present shortcomings and frustrations." The doctor found that the youngster had superior mental resources, no indications of neurological impairment or psychotic mental changes, but was emotionally quite disturbed, suffering from "lack of affection, absence of family life and rejection by a self-involved and conflicted mother."

The social worker who interviewed both Lee and Marguerite Oswald concluded that although there were indications that the boy had suffered serious personality damage, this might be repaired if he could receive help quickly. But the help never came. Available social agencies had no space for him, and when Lee Oswald became a disciplinary problem upon his return to school, the authorities considered placing him in a home for boys. Before the court took any action, however, Mrs. Oswald moved back with her son to New Orleans, where he finished ninth grade, left school to go to work and then joined the Marines.

This profile of the early life of President John F. Kennedy's assassin could be the profile of almost any delinquent youth, particularly one emerging from the slums. The Katzenbach Commission's Task Force on Juvenile Delinquency described the typical delinquent as a boy fifteen or sixteen years old, one of numerous children, who lives with his mother. His female-centered home may be broken, or may never have had a resident father, or may have a nominal male head who is simply not around or available. Whatever the cause, the typical delinquent youth usually has never known a grown man well enough to identify with or to emulate. His relations with adults and older children have been marked by alternating leniency and sternness, affection and indifference, all "in erratic and unpredictable succession." The youth's mother has little control over his comings and goings, and he may well have dropped out of school, thus having little to offer an employer.

Youngsters under eighteen years of age are responsible for approximately one-half of all serious crime committed in the United States. Fifteen-year-olds commit more such crimes than any other age group. According to recent FBI statistics, 48 per cent of all arrests for vandalism, 43 per cent of all arrests for arson, 29 per cent of all arrests for larceny and 26 per cent of all arrests for burglary involve defendants who are *under* the age of 15.

THE MAKING OF A DELINQUENT

Virtually every study of juvenile delinquency and its causes has identified family cohesiveness, including particularly supervision and discipline within the home, as the single most important factor in determining whether or not a child will violate the law. One of the best-known studies was made several years ago by Eleanor and Sheldon Glueck of Harvard University, based on an analysis of five hundred delinquent and five hundred nondelinquent youths. From their data the Gluecks produced a "Prediction Table" which could, with an alleged 70 per cent accuracy, predict future delinquency problems, and, with an alleged 85 per cent accuracy, could predict which youngsters would never present delinquency problems. Although some details of the Gluecks' conclusions have been challenged, most professionals do agree that the single ingredient of family life is the crucial factor in determining the future conduct of any child, as a youth or adult.

Interestingly, these same factors play a major role in determining susceptibility to narcotics addiction. A study of adolescent narcotics users by Professor Isidor Chein of New York University, published in 1964, affirmed earlier studies by other researchers in concluding that the single most important factor determining which youths may become narcotics addicts is the stability of family life. After probing a number of possible contributing factors, such as economic status, national origin, neighborhood environment and other variables, the Chein study deduced that family cohesion was the critical element. The NYU researchers used a fascinating series of questions in evaluating the cohesiveness of family life for the adolescents studied, covering such commonplace matters as how each teenager's family celebrated Christmas, Thanksgiving and other holidays; how the family observed birthdays; how often the family had dinner together; what the family did after dinner; whether the family went out together for visits or on picnics or on trips; how other members of the family behaved toward a member who was sick; and the frequency of family quarrels. But the place of the father in the home was the critical ingredient in its influence on addiction susceptibility. The absence of a father figure was found to be one of the most common and prominent characteristics in the background of a male addict. The patterns of criminal conduct for both youths and adults in other settings almost invariably reflect these very same deficiencies in family life as the common identifiable element shaping the personality in the direction of antisocial conduct.

Personality development is a complex process. Obviously an infant has no advance conception of society's values. The basic instincts of the newborn child are to survive and achieve satisfaction of bodily needs. Basic psychological needs also require some attention, including relationship to the mother. But no understanding of the adult world or its values or standards is possible during the very early years. Primary concentration is on the growth of the internal organs and the development of coordination and basic skills—walking, talking, playing creatively with toys and objects. When a child is two or three years of age, there are literally no controls over his conduct except those set by his parents or other adults. He smiles and is content when his needs are satisfied, and he cries and is unhappy when things are denied him or when he feels pain. An-eye-for-an-eye is his instinctive standard of moral conduct. As he grows older, the child begins to learn the the limits of what he can and cannot do through the intervention of parental rules and discipline. Scoldings and spankings become very real factors in directing the child's decision whether or not to engage in certain conduct. Slowly but surely, his personality is shaped to the rules and example of those with whom he lives and spends his days. The standards of his parents dominate his conduct as he passes through the various stages of childhood. Eventually most of those standards become his own.

When he becomes a teenager, the child is likely to go through the process of challenging and reexamining his parents' rules as a way of developing his own individual identity and independence of judgment. At this point, parental response is of major significance in shaping the values of the youth and ultimately the adult. Patience and understanding, plus consistency and firmness where appropriate, are important in helping the adolescent to reach his own decisions about right and wrong.

It is no wonder, therefore, that the stability and cohesiveness of the family are so important in shaping the young person as he progresses through his early years. Reduced to its simplest terms, the role of the parents is to set down the basic rules of conduct, both by example and by explanation; to keep an eye on compliance with those rules of conduct; and to take prompt and effective, but always fair, disciplinary action when the rules are violated. Where there is no father in the home, where there are tensions and absence of affection between parental partners, or where the parents' own standards of conduct are immoral or erratic, the process breaks down. The personality of the child is the casualty and, unfortunately, society pays the price.

We do not live in a homogeneous society, like the early tribes of Anasazi Indians in the Southwest who shared the land together, had equal access to game and corn and nuts and berries, and lived on equal footing in their cliff dwellings. Our society knows extremes in wealth, opportunity, education and environment, which can put great strains on family structure and home life. Poverty will often wear away the pride and dignity of the father, deny the family the setting for a stable home life and provide environmental forces which constantly intrude on the natural family relationship. Inadequate housing, bad schools, lack of jobs, poor health services, run-down neighborhoods; all these wear away at the chances of having a decent home life, thereby increasing dramatically the level of delinquency because the natural forces of family cohesion have been destroyed. In many ways, these individual factors can in themselves play a major role in personality development.

The public school can be an important contributing force in nurturing or destroying personality of the young. A child who comes from a poor home without books, magazines and the other incidentals of literacy most of us take for granted enters school with a distinct disadvantage. Because of their own educational handicaps, parents in poor households are unable to help with homework or even teach such basic skills as counting, saying the alphabet and learning how to tell time. On top of this, the ghetto school usually provides a harsh setting for child development. Physical surroundings are often sordid, discipline is uneven or nonexistent, fistfights and gangwars all take their toll. If the school system fails to overcome the initial handicaps which the child from a poor home brings with him, then the process of deterioration almost inevitably accelerates from that point on.

Failure is a virtual certainty. Although the youngster may be advanced each year to a higher grade, he generally has not mastered the skills assigned to him in the prior school year. At the end of one grade he may be a half year behind. Several years later he may be a year or more behind. The typical school administrator's reaction to apparent slowness in learning is to treat the child with patronizing procedures, assigning him to a class for slower students, denying him extracurricular activities, failing to help him develop worthwhile personal qualities through assigned responsibilities in the school management. The natural reaction of the student to this disparaging treatment is rebellion. The child will seek out similarly alienated students and with them turn to other diversions, creating increasing disciplinary problems. Patterns of behavior now in a serious stage of deterioration are largely the result of the school's inadequate response to deficiencies in the child over which he has no control. The end product may be a complete waste of the educational process and of the human being. As the Select Committee on Crime of the House of Representatives observed in its report on Juvenile Justice and Corrections in 1971:

> Many students who graduate from high school are functional illiterates and no better off than those who drop out and never receive an education. Neither group has very much to look forward to. Options are reduced or closed, and crime often appears as the most reasonable alternative.

The last stage along the line of influences on personality development is the job world. Many youngsters have their potential for development as useful, contributing citizens finally destroyed by the reality of unemployment. Those who have been alienated from school because of accelerating handicaps which began at home are often unable to find any job at all, much less one that pays a decent wage. The unemployment rate for youths is, in fact, several times higher than that for the general population. Today, over a *million* young people are out of school and out of work at any one time, a potential engine of human discontent and waste of alarming proportions. Those who are able to find work are limited to unskilled or semiskilled trades because of their lack of basic educational or vocational training. Union rules frequently compound the problem of access to blue-collar job opportunities, especially for minorities, so that the young person who has dropped out of school is quickly alienated from a world which offers little in the way of a future. Leaving aside the role of the schools themselves in basic job preparation, manpower-training programs have also fallen far short of the mark in opening up job opportunities for alienated young people. Even where job opportunities may exist, archaic methods of communicating such information to those in search of employment provides an additional barrier every bit as significant as that of racial discrimination or the stigma of an arrest record, a typical handicap of any youth who is a school dropout and lives in a ghetto neighborhood.

Most governmental proposals for coping with the causes of inadequate family life envision the solutions in long-range terms of better housing, schools and employment. Seldom do they offer immediate benefits for today's, or even tomorrow's, youth. We have therefore been forced to rely on other institutions and resources to deal with the problem. For several generations, private organizations such as the "Y," Boys Clubs, the Big Brothers and similar groups have provided some practical substitutes for a father in the home by taking an interest in boys from poor neighborhoods, setting them standards of decent conduct, showing an interest in their welfare and helping them get along with their peers. A basic problem with such private social service organizations is the lack of effective coordination, which results in wasteful duplication and overlapping of effort, and the spreading too thin of their financial resources. For some reason, these organizations have failed to receive the same type of financial support that some of the newer "poverty program" projects have, and many are withering away from the lack of it.

Another significant force in the community having a direct impact on the lives of young people is the policeman. As a representative of law and justice, his inadequate or insensitive conduct can do great harm in shaping the attitudes of young people. A degree of sensitivity and common sense, mixed with firmness

and fair play, can provide effective guidance and also set a valuable standard of conduct for the young. Too often, police officers
have passed the buck on handling juveniles to some special officer or group assigned the responsibility for dealing with delin-
quents. Little attention has been paid to the importance of
providing good training for all police officers who might come
into contact with youths, to avoid damagingly inept or callous
conduct. The result is that many police officers who could do
something positive to help youths only add to their alienation
and distrust.

THE JUVENILE COURTS

One of the most puzzling aspects of our present social structure is our use of the courts as the primary means for coping
with deficiencies primarily rooted in family life, in schools and
in lack of employment opportunities. Because we are devoid of
better ideas for dealing with the wayward young person, we end
up utilizing a modified criminal justice system, with all of its
inherent weaknesses and failures.

The juvenile court grew out of nineteenth-century cries for
reform in the handling of children who, until then, were treated
like adult criminals when they violated the law, and were locked
up in the same prisons and tried in the same courts. In 1861,
Illinois became the first state to appoint a special commission
that would decide minor cases against boys between the ages
of six and seventeen. Massachusetts followed in 1869 with a
special procedure for handling juvenile cases, subsequently emu-
lated by New York in 1892 and Rhode Island in 1898. The
reform movement spread rapidly, and in 1898 the Illinois legislature passed the Juvenile Court Act, establishing the first separate court especially designed to hear cases involving children.
By 1925, virtually every state had a separate juvenile court, and
today there are some 2700 juvenile courts functioning throughout the country. As part of the reform movement new descrip-
tive terms and new procedures were adopted. "Complaints"

became "petitions," "warrants" became "summonses." All other steps in the proceedings were softened, at least in name. The judge was required to sit behind a table or desk, rather than a bench. Background investigations became standard operating procedure. Lawyers were banished from the process so that adversary pressures and tactics might be avoided. Specialists were hired to diagnose delinquency and treat it almost as a disease.

Despite all these efforts at making the courts seem kindly and beneficent, the final product has been far from satisfactory. The original objectives of the reform movement have not been achieved. Delinquent young people have not been rehabilitated any more successfully than are adults in the regular criminal justice process. The courts themselves have never received adequate resources to do the job properly. The facilities available for sensitive handling of the individuals who are adjudged delinquent are limited and often harmful. The goal of rehabilitation in contrast to punishment has not been met in any significant way.

A number of special procedures have been adopted to avoid the disappointing results of the ordinary juvenile court procedures. Pretrial diversion has been employed repeatedly. An intake officer frequently functions as a representative branch of the juvenile court, intervening in each case prior to trial to determine whether the youngster should be held for judicial proceedings or diverted into some method of treatment and supervision. In many cases he may serve almost as an impartial arbiter. New York City has had some success with a similar institution called the "Youth Counsel Bureau," which enlists the help of public and private agencies in rendering assistance to young people who appear salvageable by means other than regular processing through the court. All these alternatives are, of course, a tacit recognition that the juvenile court concept itself is not the ideal vehicle for coping with young people who have not developed sufficient motivation or self-discipline to control their own conduct in a responsible fashion. The problem is that no one has yet come up with a better technique.

As it has become clear that the juvenile courts function primarily as junior criminal courts, a revolution in court procedures has taken place. Starting with the 1967 Supreme Court decision *In Re Gault*, a range of due-process requirements has been imposed on juvenile court procedure. That case grew out of the arrest of a fifteen-year-old boy on the verbal complaint of a neighbor who alleged that the boy had made an obscene telephone call. The parents of the boy never received formal notice of the proceedings. The complainant never appeared in court. None of the witnesses gave testimony under oath, or had their testimony transcribed. The youth was forced to answer questions put by the judge, and ultimately he was committed to a juvenile institution for the balance of his minority—a total of six years. The Supreme Court, characterizing the whole proceedings as "a kangaroo court," ruled that due process even in juvenile cases requires sufficient notice of court proceedings, the assistance of counsel and the constitutional protection against self-incrimination. Other recent decisions have expanded the requirements of due process so that they now largely follow those of the regular criminal courts. These recent Supreme Court rulings only underscore the split personality of the juvenile courts and the fact that they are primarily criminal courts for young people, with all the accompanying disadvantages.

The real problem with the juvenile court system, however, is not the concept of due process or adjudication, but rather the limitations on what the courts are able to do in attempting to help a delinquent youth. The principal resource is the traditional institution for detention and training of youthful offenders. There are 343 such institutions in the United States, with an inmate population of 50,000 youngsters as of June 30, 1970—42,000 in training schools, 5,000 in forestry camps and over 2,000 in diagnostic and reception centers. A study made by the U. S. Department of Health, Education and Welfare in 1971 found that more than 40 per cent of these institutions exceeded maximum recommended capacity. The average length of stay for state training schools was 9.9 months, and for all institutions 8.4 months.

Studies of these youth institutions have found them almost uniformly unsatisfactory. In New York State, for example, a 1969 survey of state training schools by the Citizens' Committee for Children found that the services needed for effective treatment and rehabilitation were not available in any of the state's fourteen training schools. Although the buildings received adequate funds and attention, little operational money was available for treatment of the inmates. Staff members lacked proper background and had no adequate in-service training. The youngsters were largely "doing time" rather than receiving educational services or treatment and guidance. The Committee also noted that all the state's training schools were located in lonely rural settings, physically and environmentally removed from the communities to which the youngsters must return, and that liaison between the training schools and the home community was weak. Because of the distance factor, families seldom were able to visit their children. The citizens' group also found inadequate after-care services, health services and mental-health services.

The House Select Committee on Crime recently inspected five youth institutions in five states, and reported in detail on both the encouraging and discouraging results of its visits. Among the institutions receiving low marks from the Committee was the Indiana Boys School at Plainfield, Indiana. That school has an attractive open campus but despite its appearance, it is overcrowded, life is regimented and drab and there is almost no community contact or involvement. The Indiana Boys School is centered on absolute discipline. Boys are told when to change their underwear. Major infractions of the rules result in solitary confinement. Boys march from class to work and live in dormitories, thirty to thirty-five boys in a row, with no privacy of any kind. Corporal punishment still exists, although it is being phased out, and boys who attempt to escape from the school are generally locked up for a minimum of seven days in maximum detention facilities—a small cell with a cot, toilet and wash basin and one book, the Bible. The Committee noted the irony of the fact that the only way boys can achieve some privacy is by being placed in maximum detention.

The Connecticut School for Boys at Meriden, Connecticut, received a similar poor rating. Although the annual allocation of $13,000 per year per boy—in contrast to $2700 a year in Indiana, and a national average of just over $5,000—would seem to indicate an enriched program, this is far from the case. Recidivism rates are 60 per cent or higher and life at the school is chaotic. A virtual civil war over treatment techniques was raging among segments of the staff. The vocational training, recreation and emphasis on security were all causes for grave concern.

The Committee also visited the Pennsylvania Industrial School at Whitehall, Pennsylvania, and found it to be close to an adult penitentiary in design and management. There was praise for the educational and vocational programs, which offer a wide range of skills, but the school was criticized for paying virtually no attention to the personality development of the inmates.

The remaining two boys' institutions visited by the House Committee were the John F. Kennedy Youth Center at Morgantown, West Virginia (an experimental Federal program based on personality classification and treatment, which the Committee found exciting and promising), and the Minnesota School for Boys at Red Wing, Minnesota. Although Morgantown received a very high rating, Red Wing seemed to provide the most hopeful signs for effective rehabilitation of any of the institutions visited by the Committee. The institution, with two hundred boys, has been undergoing a period of transformation into a new form of environment in which the youths themselves have an active role, described as "positive peer pressure." The concept was first developed experimentally at Highfields, the Lindbergh family estate in New Jersey. After a number of successful experiments with small groups, the Highfields concept was applied to larger groups at Red Wing.

The Red Wing program involves nightly confrontation sessions lasting an hour and a half among nine or ten youths under the direction of an adult leader. The boys all participate openly in a critical discussion of one another's problems and shortcomings. Emotions often run high and strong language can be heard, but the participants are encouraged to express their feelings openly and honestly. The sessions develop in each member a feeling of empathy with the others, and a desire to be helpful. In contrast to the Morgantown classification of personality groups on the basis of similarity, the groups at Red Wing are purposely mixed so that differences in personality can be utilized to help in the process of mutual and self-understanding. Boys at Red Wing live two to a room, most of them in new cottages. The youths are not handpicked to be responsive to the technique, but are assigned on a random basis as they are referred by the courts. Each of the peer groups work and attend classes together, eat and live together, providing the interaction which is the basis for the ninety-minute sessions each evening. The real test of the peer-group concept comes when a boy feels that he is ready for parole: he must obtain permission of the other members of his group as a preliminary step to asking for staff approval. There is a strong participation by outside volunteer groups in the life at Red Wing. One such group pays for the cost of clothing for the boys, selected from mail-order catalogs. Volunteer women help teach poise and manners.

Although the experiment is still fairly short-lived, the recidivism rate for those released from Red Wing has dropped from 40 per cent to less than 19 per cent after its first two years of operation under the new concept. The House Committee concluded that the techniques being used at Morgantown and Red Wing clearly hold the hope for the future as techniques for effective institutional rehabilitation of youths.

Other recent experiments in treating youthful offenders have also been encouraging. In 1966, California initiated a probation subsidy program to encourage community probationary supervision instead of institutional commitment. State officials realized that a substantial amount of money could be saved if adequate outside supervision could be utilized in place of institutionalization. Accordingly, the state offered subsidies of up to four thousand dollars per case to any county which would undertake to provide probationary supervision for youths who would otherwise be sent to a state youth institution. The program has proved extremely successful in terms of both rehabilitation and economy. Recently the community supervision approach has been refined to include differential treatment based on personality categories, similar in concept to the Morgantown, West Virginia, approach, but differing in detail. Under the California treatment program, youths are divided into nine groups based on various stages of maturity. The improved results in terms of recidivism rates have been most gratifying.

Another approach which has received favorable attention is use of the foster home. Instead of being placed in an institutional setting, youths are assigned in groups of six or seven young people to private homes located in the community, with a married couple hired to supervise them and provide a modified parental relationship. The youths attend community schools and work part time during the day, and on weekends they may visit their families. The foster parents live with the group during the week, then have the weekend off while a tutor or some other person serves in the supervisory role. Administration of such a program has obvious problems, among them the finding of suitable homes and couples who are willing to commit themselves to a twenty-four-hour job, five days a week, but the results of this approach seem well worth the effort.

GOVERNMENT AND THE FAMILY

The Katzenbach Commission estimated that 40 per cent of all male children now living in the United States would be arrested for a nontraffic offense at some time during their lives. Experience and study of patterns of youth delinquency indicate that the role of the family and related institutions has a direct impact on this percentage figure, and that if some way can be found to reduce damage to developing personalities this high level of wasted human potential might be dramatically reduced. Obviously we must do the best we can with the patchwork techniques that now exist until some better procedures are developed. But having said that, we should not throw up our hands and regard the larger task as impossible. What we are dealing with is something quite basic—the family and home life. Preachers can easily lament the passing of the older virtues and the destruction of the family as an institution, but lamenting is not what is needed. Instead, we should stop being so hesitant about trying to grapple with the problem and should immediately begin the search for ways to make the family stronger and to provide a more realistic substitute when it breaks down.

It is self-evident that government cannot make a husband and wife love each other or show affection toward their children, but government does have a role to play in providing support services for the family, and more attention should be given to that function than has been the case so far. Family stability and more adequate family home life can be encouraged by such devices as income tax policies and direct financial aid. Even more basic is the potential role of government in providing family planning services so that those who do not want the responsibility of another child are enabled to make a free choice. Schools could not only respond better to the needs of the disadvantaged child, but they could also work more closely with the family as a unit by encouraging a greater interest in the child's development and closer bonds between home and school. Many other government services, of course, also have a significant effect on family life; these would include provision of recreation facilities, and various programs of family counseling, health care and, above all, welfare.

In 1971, the Citizens' Committee for Children in New York released a study reviewing the twenty-five-year history of welfare assistance to dependent children and came to the conclusion that an entirely new concept was needed. Briefly, CCC proposed the assignment of primary responsibility in providing family services to locally based general Family Service Social Workers, who would operate out of neighborhood offices and would work closely with various social service agencies in the community. The major emphasis would be on providing personal and family help when and where needed. The objective would be easy accessibility and a continuing relationship between each family and its social worker. The social worker would in his or her way have a similar relationship with the family as the family doctor, there to help when needed and counted on as a friend.

It is not hard to find specific measures that would ameliorate the present situation. The Katzenbach Commission came up with a most impressive list of practical proposals which would undoubtedly improve the juvenile court system greatly. But what is absent is emphasis on providing the missing ingredient in family life that caused inadequate personality development in the first place. Reliance on artificial court structures, revolving-door probation services and short-order counseling is no real substitute. Somehow we must find a way to strengthen the family, improve the role of both parents (or provide a meaningful substitute) and insure that the outside environment in which the child grows up—especially that of the school—supports the child's needs in a constructive way. By the time he winds up in juvenile court, it is usually too late.

Chapter 13

Automobile Accidents: Who Are the Real Victims?

WHEN the New York State Legislature adjourned its 1972 session without acting to reduce the volume of automobile accident cases clogging the civil courts, Governor Nelson A. Rockefeller lashed out at the state's legal profession for preventing passage of a "no-fault" automobile-accident-insurance measure which would have provided payment for many accident claims without the need for ever going to court. The Governor accused the lawyers of bringing "inordinate pressures" to block passage of the bill, declaring:

> This was shocking evidence of minorities imposing their will on the majority through pressure, personal attacks and threats of political retaliation in an election year.

The Albany correspondent for *The New York Times* identified the New York State Trial Lawyers Association as the principal lobbying group responsible for killing the no-fault measure, which had been supported by every consumer group in the state. Early in the session, the *Times* reported, one of the bill's sponsors had conducted an informal canvass and concluded that he had a majority of the members of the Senate ready to vote for the bill. "But the word got out," he asserted, "and within twenty-four hours *they* were up here."

"They" were the trial lawyers, who fanned out through the

State Capitol, collaring senators and assemblymen in the corridors and reportedly threatening some of them with political reprisals if they did not vote to defeat the no-fault measure. Various legislators who had originally agreed to support the reform proposal quietly backed off under the pressure. Three hundred trial lawyers worked steadily to remind the members of the legislature that they carried a lot of weight back home, where they belonged to county bar associations, the Rotary and local political clubs. Commented one state senator, "They can bring a lot of heat on a guy in a shaky district." The tactics proved effective. By the time the Legislature adjourned, the no-fault insurance proposal was dead.

The reason for the battle over no-fault automobile insurance becomes apparent from a look at what is involved. In New York State alone, automobile accidents result in 1 person being killed every 3 hours—a total of 9 killed every day. One person is injured in New York State every 1½ minutes; 970 each day. A pedestrian is hit by a motor vehicle about every 18 minutes— that is 82 pedestrians hit every day, 30 of them children under 15 years of age. During the course of the year, 1 vehicle out of every 9 is involved in an accident. Over the course of the last 40 years the number of persons injured in automobile accidents has climbed drastically, although the number of people killed in such accidents has remained almost constant. According to New York State figures, 2,984 persons were killed in automobile accidents in 1930, as compared with 3,200 in 1969. The number of persons injured in automobile accidents in 1930 was 121,372, while the number injured in 1969 had tripled to 353,944. The number of motor vehicles registered in New York also tripled, from 2,360,668 in 1930, to 6,991,530 in 1969. In terms of insurance premiums, recoveries and lawyers' fees, these statistics represent a lot of money.

Nationally, the impact of the motor vehicle and motor vehicle accidents has been staggering, and the cost of automobile insurance has spiraled. During the four years prior to 1971, property damage claims climbed 38 per cent, while the average claim for personal injuries went up 32 per cent. The cost of liability insurance for automobile owners has risen in every state during the past ten years, with an average increase in premiums of 76 per cent.

What has really prompted the movement toward no-fault insurance has been the waste of money involved in determining who is at fault and must pay the damages. A recent study by the Senate Antitrust and Monopoly Subcommittee concluded that out of every dollar paid for automobile liability insurance relating to bodily injury, eighteen cents goes to insurance salesmen, sixteen cents to insurance company overhead and other expenses, twenty-four cents to lawyers' fees and court costs, and only forty-two cents is paid out in benefits to accident victims. This dissipation of the insurance dollar, together with other grievances against the handling of automobile accident claims, finally provided the steam for a series of actions to develop new automobile-accident insurance plans in various states. The essential concept of the most common reform plan—no-fault insurance—is that everyone injured in an accident should receive compensation, no matter who caused the accident.

The first American jurisdiction to adopt no-fault insurance was Puerto Rico, which put its plan into operation at the beginning of 1970. Up until that time, it was estimated that nine out of ten accident victims in Puerto Rico received no compensation for their injuries. No-fault insurance became compulsory for all vehicle owners, and since its enactment all medical and hospital bills are now paid by a government insurance agency. Prescribed payments are also made for dismemberment, death, lost wages and "pain and suffering." Prior to the enactment of the no-fault plan, insurance premiums in Puerto Rico were the sixth highest in the United States, but upon adoption of the plan the premiums were cut by 30 per cent. Annual coverage now costs a motorist thirty-five dollars.

The first mainland program of no-fault insurance was enacted in Massachusetts and went into effect on January 1, 1971. Under the Massachusetts law, all motor vehicle owners must carry bodily-injury insurance. The insurance company is then obligated to pay claims of up to two thousand dollars per person for medical costs, plus lost wages at a rate of 75 per cent of the victim's weekly pay. This money would go to people riding with the insured, or to pedestrians whom he may have injured. Extra coverage is available if desired. One of the controversial features of the Massachusetts law is that it rules out recovery for one popular basis of much automobile litigation—"pain and suffering"—unless the injured person incurs at least five hundred dollars' worth of medical expenses, or the injury results in death, dismemberment, permanent disfigurement, loss of sight or hearing, or a fracture. Initial results under the Massachusetts statute have been dramatic. The number of claims for bodily injury has dropped sharply, and instead of a predicted increase in insurance premiums by approximately 20 per cent, the premiums actually have been reduced by 15 per cent.

Some of the other states which followed closely on the Massachusetts plan were Delaware, with no-fault coverage paying up to ten thousand dollars for medical expenses, loss of earnings and the like; Florida, with no-fault coverage up to five thousand dollars, subject to certain limits; Illinois, with no-fault payments of medical expenses up to two thousand dollars, and lost wages up to one hundred and fifty dollars per week for a maximum of one year; Oregon, with no-fault coverage of three thousand dollars for medical expenses and six thousand dollars for lost wages; and South Dakota, with an optional no-fault program with coverage of two thousand dollars for medical expenses and sixty dollars per week for up to one year of lost wages, plus a death benefit of ten thousand dollars. Connecticut has recently joined the list. Many other states have also been working on no-fault legislation, and Senator Philip A. Hart of Michigan has proposed Federal legislation that would require each state to adopt a program meeting certain minimum standards. In its 1973 session, the New York legislature finally adopted a no-fault bill which bars going to court unless medical expenses exceed $500 or extreme injuries are involved.

Part of the premise behind no-fault insurance legislation has been the ever-increasing importance of the automobile in American life and the number of accidents affecting American families. Four out of every five families now own an automobile, and almost every driver will be involved in at least one motor vehicle accident during his lifetime. State Insurance Department actuaries predict that 24 per cent of all drivers will be involved in at least one motor vehicle accident in the course of one year, 56 per cent in the course of three years, 75 per cent in the course of five years, 94 per cent in the course of ten years and 99-plus per cent in the course of twenty years. Over the course of a year some 56,000 people are killed in automobile accidents, and another 4.6 million are injured. The average driver has a better-than-even chance of having an accident every three years.

Prior to no-fault insurance, the sole procedure for compensating automobile-accident victims was through determination that the other party involved in the accident was to blame. This concept goes back to horse-and-buggy days, when the American legal system evolved a set of principles under which a person must be found to have been in the wrong before the person he injures can obtain any recovery against him. If fault cannot be established, then there is no legal basis for awarding damages. Moreover, if it can be demonstrated that the injured person was guilty of "contributory negligence," then he is barred from recovery even though the person who caused the accident was at fault. Although there might have been some useful social purpose behind this concept when it first was applied and when the person found to be at fault had to compensate the victim out of his own pocket, the evolution of automobile liability insurance has totally changed the circumstances. The process of adjudicating fault has become primarily a tactic for delaying the payment of claims as long as possible, rather than an attempt at ensuring justice for an innocent driver. Today the driver who is found negligent does not personally pay the damages; instead, his insurance company makes the payment out of the premiums paid in by all of the drivers who have taken out policies with that particular insurer. The fault concept, therefore, has lost its validity, but it continues on as a legal anachronism because that is the way the whole thing began. Indeed, the fiction is continued in the courtroom, where everyone goes through the motions of pretending that the driver is defending the lawsuit, when in fact the lawyers are paid by the insurance company and are there to protect the company's interest against having to pay the claim. It is still reversible error for the plaintiff to bring to the attention of the jury the fact that the defendant is covered by insurance, despite the fact that there is not a juror anywhere today who does not know that an insurance company will pay the judgment if it is rendered.

Court congestion has been aggravated by the flood of automobile-accident cases—some two hundred thousand new cases each year. Delays in the judicial process have resulted in the postponement of settlement discussions until the cases are about to go to trial. The victim, meanwhile, must wait several years before he can expect to receive any form of payment, and the pressure from the delay, plus the uncertainties generated by the law, build up a desire to settle cheaply rather than prolong the process. Added costs include the fees for both plaintiff's and defendant's lawyers, who must go through all the steps of gathering evidence, conducting depositions, having photographs taken, retaining medical experts to make examinations and the like. When the victim finally does receive some compensation for his injuries and expenses, a substantial proportion of it goes to his lawyer. It cannot be denied that the plaintiff's counsel must put in a substantial amount of professional work and judgment in investigating and preparing his client's case, and therefore deserves to be compensated for that work. The question that should be asked, however, is whether it is *necessary* for that work to be done at all.

In New York State, one out of every four persons injured in automobile accidents did not receive any compensation under the fault system. Even where payment was made, the delay in payment was far greater than in any other form of insurance protection. The New York State Insurance Department compiled the following table showing the interval between the making of claims and payment for selected lines of insurance:

Interval Between Claim and Payment	Auto Bodily Injury Liability	Auto Physical Damage	Home-owners	Burglary	Individual Accident and Health
2 months or less	23%	79%	92%	64%	98%
6 months or less	49	98	99	97	99
1 year or less	71	99	99	99	100
2 years or less	83	100	100	99	—
3 years or less	88	—	—	100	—
Average period (months)	15.8	1.5	1.6	1.9	0.4

An average delay of almost sixteen months in paying automobile claims under an insurance system which is compulsory is hard to justify. Even more troublesome was the fact that 12 per cent of the claims, usually representing the most serious injuries, still had not been paid three years after the accident.

The impact of these accident cases on court congestion is serious. A 1971 study of delay in personal injury jury cases in state trial courts, compiled by New York University's Institute of Judicial Administration, found that more than 20 per cent of the courts in the major metropolitan areas in the country had trial delays of more than two and a half years in personal injury cases, some of them running as long as four or five years. Among the most extreme examples of delay found were the following:

Court and County	Population	Elapsed Time from Service of Answer to Trial (Average in Months)
Circuit Court, Cook County (Chicago) Illinois	5,427,237	61.7
Supreme Court, Bronx County (Bronx) New York	1,441,403	61.5
Supreme Court, Rockland County (Rockland) New York	228,897	56.3
Supreme Court, Kings County (Brooklyn) New York	2,562,245	51.9

Supreme Court, New York County (Manhattan) New York	1,509,327	49.9
Supreme Court, Westchester County (White Plains) New York	888,314	49.6
Court of Common Pleas, Philadelphia County (Philadelphia) Pennsylvania	1,927,863	46.8
Supreme Court, Nassau County (Mineola) New York	1,413,012	43.8
Supreme Court, Queens County (Queens) New York	1,964,147	42.0

Some lawyers challenge the impact of personal-injury litigation in generating delay in the courts. They say that personal-injury cases consume only 17 per cent of the court time in the nation's trial system. What this argument overlooks, however, is that the 17 per cent is "judge time" spent presiding over those cases which actually go to trial. Most personal-injury cases never do go to trial. Yet hundreds of thousands of these cases clog up court calendars and prevent other cases from being reached for trial as they are processed through various court steps, conferences and calendar calls, only to be finally settled on the eve of trial, often many years after the accident happened. The 17 per cent of courtroom time is only the tip of the iceberg, representing about 1 per cent of all automobile liability claims. The other 99 per cent of the cases are settled without trial, usually after long delay.

No-fault insurance theoretically is designed to eliminate most of these problems in the present automobile-accident compensation system. As it has evolved, however, the program has resulted in a series of compromises, so that it only applies in a limited class of cases, usually involving quite small amounts. These smaller cases, however, when handled in volume, can add up to quite significant bread and butter for many claimants' attorneys.

A trial lawyer from Los Angeles, writing in the *American Bar Association Journal* in July, 1972, charged that the real backers of no-fault insurance were the insurance companies themselves, out to make higher profits. The lawyer painted a vivid picture of the legal profession guarding the "blameless accident victim from being carved up as a sacrificial lamb by the insurance industry on the altar of higher profits." He also complained that it was not a fair contest to pit a profession of privately practicing lawyers against a forty-billion-dollar industry that has access to "all channels of mass communication."

The most vigorous opponents of no-fault insurance have been the members of the American Trial Lawyers Association, made up primarily of lawyers who specialize in motor vehicle personal-injury litigation. A recent issue of the Association's *Journal* described the Illinois no-fault insurance legislation as "Legalized Consumer Fraud." That same issue included a lengthy article by Craig Spangenberg, chairman of the Association's Auto Reparation's Committee, vigorously attacking the proposed Federal no-fault legislation. The basic thesis of Mr. Spangenberg's attack was this:

> The fault system rests on the bedrock concept that there is a difference between right and wrong, and if one man carelessly injures his fellow man by wrongful conduct, the innocent victim ought to be compensated for *all* his losses, and the wrong doer should be liable for the losses he has caused by violating the rule of careful conduct.

Mr. Spangenberg condemned the proposed Federal no-fault plan for abolishing "every natural right and every legal right of the American motorist."

To counter the no-fault movement, the American Trial Lawyers Association has also devised its own plan for protecting the insured motorist, which it called a "Fair Pay Plan." This proposal includes Federal regulation of the automobile insurance industry, supervision of insurance company investments and profits, mandatory increases in insurance coverage, prohibition against canceling of insurance policies and other similar suggestions. There are seeds of merit in some of these ideas, but not one of them really answers the most serious deficiencies in the present system of compensation for motor vehicle injuries —delay and waste.

Not all associations of lawyers in the United States have opposed reforming the present inefficient and antiquated method of handling automobile-accident cases. A special committee of the Association of the Bar of the City of New York, which was headed by David W. Peck and included several former bar association presidents among its members, issued a report in February, 1972, urging much more sweeping reforms than even those incorporated in the proposed no-fault legislation. The Peck Committee totally rejected the idea that the fault concept of compensation acted to deter or punish the wrongdoer, pointing out that the existence of mandatory insurance makes certain that the person at fault will never have to pay out of his own pocket. The Committee also itemized eight separate defects in the existing automobile liability system: the difficulty of determining fault, the denial of compensation to many victims, slowness in payment of claims, the fact that settlements are a compromise and not directly related to injuries, the overcompensation of trivial claims and the undercompensation of serious ones, the frequent payment of duplicate benefits where an injured person has his own accident or hospitalization insurance, the waste of money for uneconomic functions instead of compensating the injured person, and the clogging of the courts with automobile cases. The Committee recommended a four-point program:

1. Abolition of the right of action based on negligence.

2. Compulsory insurance for owners of motor vehicles to compensate for injuries to occupants of the vehicle, to pedestrians and to property resulting from accidents.

3. Insurance coverage to include all net economic loss of the injured persons, with payment to be made periodically as needed to cover medical expenses, loss of income, rehabilitation and other proper expenses. Scheduled payments for specific perma-

nent injuries, but none for those which are not capable of objective determination.

4. Avoidance of duplication of benefits.

One special feature of automobile-accident litigation is the widespread use of "contingent" fees, in which compensation depends on a successful result. Theoretically these fees, which tend to be quite large, are justified by the risk the lawyer takes, but in actuality most established personal-injury lawyers will not accept a case unless the liability is clear and the payment of damages is assured. A study conducted by the U. S. Department of Transportation disclosed that the average contingent fee is over 35 per cent, and that in some cases it may rise to more than 50 per cent of the amount of recovery. There have been criticisms of the contingent fee as producing a conflict of interest between the attorney and his client, encouraging exploitation of damages for pain and suffering, fraudulent puffing of claims and other unethical conduct.

The general feeling in the legal profession seems to be that no-fault insurance will become a reality in one form or another. But those whose livelihoods are directly involved are understandably not very happy at the prospect. As one Boston lawyer observed about the reaction of local attorneys to the Massachusetts no-fault insurance legislation: "I guess those lawyers must feel like the blacksmith who woke up one morning to see the Model T go by his window."

Chapter 14

Business and the Law—
The Price May Be Too High

IN the fall of 1920, humorist Will Rogers received a letter from a Wall Street corporation lawyer threatening him with a Federal Trade Commission proceeding for "unfair competition." Rogers, who was in Hollywood at the time making motion pictures, had recently finished a series of short subjects on current topics called the "Illiterate Digest." On behalf of Funk & Wagnalls Company, which published a weekly periodical called *The Literary Digest* and also produced short subjects which drew on material taken from the *Digest*, the lawyer claimed that Rogers' parody was lowering the prestige of his client's publication and demanded that Rogers withdraw the use of the objectionable title or face the consequences.

Rogers' reply was a classic:

Los Angeles, Cal.,
Nov. 15, 1920.

MR. WM BEVERLY WINSLOW,

Dear Sir,

Your letter in regard to my competition with the Literary Digest received and I never felt as swelled up in my life, And am glad you wrote directly to me instead of communicating with my Lawyers, As I have not yet reached that stage of

prominence where I was commiting unlawful acts and re-
quireing a Lawyer, Now if the Literary Digest feels that the
competition is to keen for them—to show you my good sports-
manship I will withdraw, In fact I had already quit as the
gentlemen who put it out were behind in their payments and
my humor kinder waned, in fact after a few weeks of no
payments I couldent think of a single joke. And now I want
to inform you truly that this is the first that I knew my Title
of the Illiterate Digest was an infringement on yours as they
mean the direct opposite, If a magazine was published called
Yes and another Bird put one out called No I suppose he
would be infringeing. But you are a Lawyer and its your business to change the meaning of words, so I lose before I start,

Now I have not written for these people in months and
they havent put any gags out unless it is some of the old ones
still playing. If they are using gags that I wrote on topical
things 6 months ago then I must admit that they would be
in competition with the ones the Literary Digest Screen uses
now. I will gladly furnish you with their address, in case you
want to enter suit, And as I have no Lawyer you can take my
case too and whatever we get out of them we will split at the
usual Lawyer rates of 80-20, the client of course getting the
20,

Now you inform your Editors at once that their most
dangerous rival has withdrawn, and that they can go ahead
and resume publication, But you inform Your clients that if
they ever take up Rope Throwing or chewing gum that I will
consider it a direct infringement of my rights and will protect
it with one of the best gun-toting Lawyers in Oklahoma,

Your letter to me telling me I was in competition with the
Digest would be just like Harding writing to Cox and telling
him he took some of his votes,

So long Beverly if you ever come to California, come out
to Beverly where I live and see me

Illiterately yours
WILL ROGERS.

Far too few business controversies end on such a light note.
Many of them wind up in court, and when they do, it is usually
no laughing matter.

Representing business clients is a major part of the work of
the legal profession, and hearing business cases is a substantial

part of the work of the courts. Indeed, properly functioning courts, by providing a forum for the prompt resolution of business disputes, are an absolutely essential part of a free and competitive economy. A substantial amount of judicial time is spent hearing cases involving contract disputes, real property questions, antitrust actions, copyright, patent and trademark matters, tax litigation and other legal controversies which go to the heart of American business operations. In theory, at least, the courts are ideally suited for this function. Judges generally have excellent training, broad experience and enough exposure to complicated questions in their work so that they can confront business questions without being overwhelmed by them, and work out practical solutions. Where judges are below an adequate level of professional competence, of course, business litigants suffer in the same way as any other petitioners. But where they are reasonably capable, they usually can meet the problems brought to them with intelligence and fairness. In actual practice, however, the overall judicial process has become so cumbersome and expensive that it is not really prudent for a businessman to bring a dispute to the courts for resolution unless its judicial resolution is of such crucial importance that expense does not matter. Even then the process is usually wasteful and exasperating.

Most business disputes are generally based on misunderstanding. Almost invariably there has been a lack of communication somewhere—a failure of the parties to reach prior agreement on the particular question involved. Difficulties in communicating are inherent in most human relations, and are summed up well in a sign on the office wall of one New York lawyer:

> I know you believe you understood what you think I said, but I am not sure you realize that what you heard is not what I meant.

Businessmen anxious to complete a deal do not bother to focus on potential problems they do not believe will arise, or if they do deal with them, they do not take the trouble to write down their intentions clearly. Later, when something goes wrong, there is usually a significant gap between what the parties really intended. Since one party is likely to lose money depending on how the dispute comes out, the misunderstanding hardens into controversy and, too often, litigation.

A good practical lawyer, when he is consulted about a business dispute, will usually try to get to the heart of the problem quickly and then sit down with the other side to see if the controversy cannot be resolved before the positions become rigid. Sadly, not many lawyers follow this course. This is not to suggest that lawyers deliberately stir up or prolong litigation out of a venal desire to get larger fees. It is simply that they have no particular motivation to affirmatively go out and try to achieve an out-of-court solution when their clients have not been able to attain that result on their own. They are hired to handle a lawsuit, and handle a lawsuit they will. Most lawyers start getting seriously interested in working out the settlement of a business dispute only when they are about to have to go to trial. At that point, the possibility of losing the client's case begins to loom large, and a settlement is the last clear chance to protect against any such unfortunate result. In addition, of course, the delay and expense of litigation has undoubtedly turned the client's own thoughts toward settling at a reasonable figure.

Even before reaching the trial, a great deal of time and money can go into the preliminary stages of a business litigation. Most large legal firms which engage in corporation law automatically utilize the full range of available pretrial motions, interrogatories, depositions and other preliminary procedures. Although many of these tools can be useful in fact-gathering, they also tend to wear out the opposition and add a severe financial burden. They therefore serve as important—and expensive—tactical weapons in business cases.

Lawyers are usually compensated on an hourly basis for the time they spend in commercial litigation. In most law firms it is customary to keep a "diary" of the hours spent on each matter, usually broken down into quarter-hour units. The quarter-hours add up quickly, and they are multiplied by varying hourly rates depending on the level in the firm's hierarchy of the lawyer who does the work. A junior lawyer, fairly fresh out of law school, may come quite cheap, while the time of a senior partner may run to one hundred or two hundred dollars an hour.

Abraham Lincoln once wrote to a client sending back part of the fee he had been paid:

> I have just received yours of the 16th, with check of Flagg & Savage for twenty-five dollars. You must think I am a high-priced man. You are too liberal with your money. Fifteen dollars is enough for the job. I send you a receipt for fifteen dollars, and return to you a ten dollar bill.

Not many letters of that sort get written today. It is not unusual for litigation expenses of a major corporation to run to several hundred thousand dollars a year in legal fees alone. These fees, of course, do not simply go into the lawyer's pocket. They also go to pay high office rents, salaries of secretaries, messengers, telephone operators, file clerks and younger associates, and law library expenses.

Dissatisfaction with the handling of business litigation in the courts a generation ago produced a reform movement which resulted in the adoption of "liberalized" discovery rules and practice. The movement began in the Federal courts in the 1940's, and has since spread now to the state courts as well. The basic concept of the reformers was to eliminate the surprise factor from litigation, so that cases did not depend so much on a game of wits and professional skill in the courtroom, but instead might be better adjudicated after all the facts had been fully aired through pretrial discovery. Essentially the idea was a good one, and there can be no doubt that when an effective job of taking testimony of witnesses and examining documents has been done, both parties are much better to appraise their own situation and the strengths and weaknesses of their case. Pretrial depositions, however, involve not only fees for lawyers on both sides, but also the high costs of stenographic transcripts. The same result could obviously be achieved on a more informal basis, and at much less expense, if lawyers would only spend more effort trying to reach fair appraisals of their respective claims without the formalities of the discovery process or the petty tactical maneuvering involved.

It is not at all unusual for the lawyers on one side of a hard-fought business litigation to serve motion papers late on a Friday afternoon which require the other side to be in court with answering papers on the following Monday. What this means, of course, is that the other lawyers have to work through the weekend. You can guess who pays the bill. This type of petty imposition on fellow lawyers, combined with deliberate misuse of the discovery process as a tactical device to harass opponents or gain some other special advantage, is one indication of what is wrong with the present method of business litigation. Not all lawyers engaged in business litigation deliberately misuse pretrial procedures. Some, on the other hand, neglect the rules entirely, thereby doing a disservice to their clients. But there are too many occasions where unnecessary papers are served, unnecessary motions made and unnecessary tactical maneuvers employed. One has only to visit a Motion Part in a busy metropolitan court and listen to the petty disputes between lawyers over the most insignificant procedural controversies to realize that something is wrong.

Close observers have described the drawn-out bankruptcy proceedings of the Penn Central Railroad as "a lawyer's dream." There have been court hearings with more than a hundred lawyers present. One attorney for the SEC commented, "It's like peeling an onion. For each skin of the onion you need a new lawyer." Quipped *The New York Times*: "The Penn Central may not be the best railroad in the world, but it is a gravy train for lawyers."

Many businessmen have come to realize that business litigation can be terribly expensive, and the outcome not very certain. Experienced businessmen increasingly avoid getting involved with the courts in the first place, and just abandon their claims without bothering to have them resolved. The reason was delightfully stated in another context by Roger Bryant Hunting in a parody on Hamlet's soliloquy:

> To sue, or not to sue; that is the question:
> Whether 'tis meet to suffer
> The pain and damage of the outrageous collision,
> Or to take action against the author of my troubles,
> And by suing end them?
> It gives me pause. There's the respect
> That makes calamity of so long life;
> The dread of the law's delay,
> The undiscovered temple of Justice from whose bourn
> No litigant returns without a puzzled mind,
> Makes me rather bear those ills I have
> Than fly to others I know not of.

Litigation expense by itself is an important makeweight in deciding whether to go to court or settle a business claim. A conversation between lawyer and client may run something like this: "It will cost you fifty thousand dollars to defend this case through the courts. You can settle it for fifteen thousand. What do you want to do?"

One of the factors that makes business litigation expensive is the factor of delay resulting from the availability of a jury trial at the request of either party, unless the case is purely equitable in nature and the plaintiff is seeking an injunction or accounting and no damages, in which case it is only heard by a judge. Because of competition for trial juries as a result of the large numbers of cases involving automobile accidents, business litigation must often wait a long time before being reached for trial. Demands for a jury, therefore, have become a tactical device to prolong litigation, thereby increasing costs for the other side and, consequently, the settlement value of the claim. Former Chief Judge J. Edward Lumbard of the U. S. Court of Appeals for the Second Circuit recently pointed out that trial by jury in civil cases has become very rare in England because of Acts of Parliament which limit jury trials to cases of libel, slander, malicious prosecution, false imprisonment, seduction or breach of promise, or where the court specifically orders it. During a recent three-year period, only 4 per cent of the trials in London were heard by a jury, while less than one-half of 1 per cent of the cases outside London were jury cases. Judge

Lumbard notes that jury trials are more deeply imbedded in the American tradition, largely because of our method of selecting judges. English judges traditionally have more independence and hence more freedom from political pressures. Most American judges are elected, and as a result are at least apparently susceptible to outside interference. American litigants, therefore, would not willingly give up the protection of having a trial jury available to decide the facts impartially and objectively. Nonetheless, it has been repeatedly argued that jury trials are not suitable for complicated business cases. Most jurors must be educated on basic issues, frequently requiring expenditures of time and money for expert witnesses. Inefficient administration of the courts and jury system, frequent adjournments and calendar congestion all generate pressure on the parties to settle. This potential abuse of the jury system and the litigation process makes it possible for litigants to bring claims purely for their nuisance value.

One of the most notorious areas for nuisance claims is that of stockholder litigation. There is a hard-core group of lawyers who specialize in bringing suits against corporate officers and directors. Where these claims are valid, they render an important service to the public and to the stockholders. But where the claims are lacking in real merit, such litigation becomes nothing more than a respectable form of blackmail. Since the corporation's directors and officers invariably are anxious to have such claims settled promptly to avoid possible personal embarrassment, the stockholder's lawyer can anticipate a settlement offer that will assure him a handsome fee. Generally speaking, such fees start at a minimum of twenty thousand dollars. Through various procedural devices, the stockholder's attorney can always keep the case going until he receives a settlement offer which will assure the fee he wants.

Unfortunately, it is possible for the lawyer's interest in his fee to create a conflict of interest. Sometimes meritorious claims are settled for less than their true worth because the plaintiff's lawyer is being so handsomely compensated in the settlement that he is just as anxious to have the case end as are the

corporate officers and directors. Even if the attorney is successful at trial, he is not likely to get as generous a fee as might be
offered in settlement, and therefore he is prepared to work with
the defendants' lawyers to have the case concluded promptly.
There is a procedure for sending out notices to other stockholders before such a stockholders' derivative suit can be settled,
but the effectiveness of this technique is open to serious doubt.
Too often it serves to attract a dissident stockholder motivated solely by the prospect of earning a fee for his attorney.
Undoubtedly there are many cases that are handled in the most
complete good faith, with the interest of the public and the
stockholders paramount, but there are enough potential abuses
to raise serious doubts as to the integrity of the process as a
whole.

Several years ago, a new technique was developed to side-
step court litigation through the use of arbitration. The American Arbitration Association was established for the express purpose of resolving commercial controversies. Many agreements
now provide that if a dispute should arise under the contract,
it will be submitted to arbitration rather than to the courts.
Such an agreement is enforceable, and if one party tries to sue
instead, the other can move to have the matter sent to arbitration. Under the arbitration practice, each party sets forth its
respective claims informally. Then a list of prospective arbitrators
is circulated to the parties, who indicate which names on the
list are satisfactory. The marked lists of prospective arbitrators
are then compared by AAA administrative personnel and those
arbitrators who appear to be satisfactory to both sides are selected to sit on the panel. After that, the facts are presented
for decision.

All of this sounds very simple and attractive. In smaller disputes, arbitration is probably a good alternative to court litigation, but in a complicated case involving substantial amounts
of money, arbitration has many drawbacks. The process can be
very slow. Since arbitrators, if they are any good, are usually
busy people, it is frequently hard to arrange for them to sit
except on intermittent days over the course of many weeks or

months. On top of that, the arbitrators are not experienced as judges or lawyers, but rather are people versed in the particular industry or field. Businessmen are accustomed to working out compromises between conflicting viewpoints. In contrast, lawyers and judges are trained to decide a question one way or the other based on the facts and the law. Arbitration often results in compromise decisions which tend to divide the respective claims in half. As a result, nobody wins, nobody loses and nobody is very happy.

ANTITRUST ENFORCEMENT

The basic problem with court enforcement of the antitrust laws is not so much in the courts, but in the enforcement agencies themselves. Antitrust cases are extremely complicated; to investigate and prosecute them in court is extremely time-consuming. Corporate defendants invariably are represented by the highest-priced legal talent, who are skilled in procedures and maneuvers which will slow down even the most energetic government attorneys. The budget for the Antitrust Division of the Department of Justice and for the Federal Trade Commission is extremely limited. The ability of these agencies to pursue violators of the antitrust laws is sharply curtailed by the dearth of staff attorneys available to do the job. This means that enforcement must be selective rather than comprehensive.

But there is something else at work, too, and that is the bureaucratic nature of the enforcement machinery. Unlike local U. S. Attorneys' or District Attorneys' offices which draw on young lawyers as raw manpower and provide intensive trial experience in the courtroom, the Antitrust Division and the FTC are manned primarily by career lawyers, who too often come to realize that cases never move very quickly and there is no point in developing ulcers worrying about it. This is not to say that there are not many extremely capable, dedicated lawyers in the Antitrust Division and the FTC, but the prevailing philosophy is that a case which cannot be dealt with today can just as easily be put off until tomorrow. Certainly such problems pertain not only to these agencies, but apply to most large government law offices which do not have regular staff turnover. The combination of staff shortages plus bureaucratic slow motion has meant that the antitrust laws have not been implemented to their fullest potential.

When they are used, the antitrust laws can be very effective. The prosecution of corporate officers for price-fixing in the electrical industry a few years ago stunned the American business world, and similar shocks ought to be repeated at regular intervals. Recent enforcement efforts against mergers by large corporations have also been very successful. The number of corporate mergers climbed from 1,950 in 1964 to 6,107 in 1969. Then the Department of Justice initiated a crackdown against business conglomerates, and the number of mergers dropped to 5,152 in 1970, and to 4,608 in 1971. That is a good result. Meanwhile, of course, because of the shortage of personnel, this has meant that enforcement efforts against other monopolistic practices and price-fixing have had to suffer.

In June, 1971, a team of investigators under the direction of Ralph Nader produced a 1,148-page report, *The Closed Enterprise System,* which charged that lax, inefficient and politically influenced enforcement of the antitrust laws costs consumers between forty-eight and sixty billion dollars per year in higher prices. Among the report's recommendations were enactment of new legislation to permit the breaking up of large corporations; public reporting of meetings between businessmen and government officials to discuss antitrust cases; and authorization for the chief of the Antitrust Division to initiate proceedings without the specific approval of the Attorney General. The study also proposed that the penalties for criminal violation of the antitrust laws be augmented to provide a minimum jail term and an increase in fines. Calling for new legislation outlawing further mergers by the five hundred largest industrial corporations, as well as the breakup of "shared monopolies" in industries with only a few principal companies in control, the

report concluded by urging the elimination of price-fixing under
state "fair trade" laws and the creation of a single "Competition
Protective Agency" out of a merger of the Antitrust Division
and the FTC. Many of the criticisms in the Nader report were
not entirely fair, but one most significant and meaningful recommendation would have Congress increase the budget for antitrust enforcement by five times, from the present twenty million
dollars per year to a total of one hundred million dollars
annually. That would accomplish something. There can be no
doubt that emphasis on increased enforcement budgets is sound.
Vigorous enforcement of the trust laws can produce useful and
healthy results for the benefit of the general public, but they
cannot occur if the laws go unused because there are not enough
investigators or trial lawyers to develop the cases.

SECURITIES LAW ENFORCEMENT

Another enforcement area of significance to the business
community comes under the jurisdiction of the Securities and
Exchange Commission. The courts are perfectly capable of acting effectively to enforce the securities laws, provided the cases
are properly developed and promptly presented for adjudication. But the SEC is woefully short of manpower to do an
adequate job, lacking enough staff even to cover minimal investigations of the securities industry. Such enforcement action
that is taken must necessarily be selective. When the cases reach
litigation, they are frequently comprised, often in a fashion
which raises grave doubts as to what has been accomplished.

The usual SEC settlement of a securities case involves the
signing of a consent decree, sometimes even before the case is
filed, under which the defendant promises to obey the law.
Such a mild reprimand is hardly a way of developing respect
for the securities laws. Indeed, this approach is regarded almost
with derision by many segments of the securities industry. One
might well ask what is the point of going through all the effort

of investigating a violation of the securities laws, catching someone red-handed and then simply saying, "Please don't do that
again."

Here, too, the principal remedy is increased budgetary allot-
ments for the hiring of investigators and lawyers to look into
securities violations, bring them to court and prosecute them
vigorously. But in the case of the SEC, something more is
needed. Policy in litigation is set by the members of the Commission, who review every case in detail and who too often give
the effect of showing considerable protectiveness toward the
securities dealers, corporate officers and others involved in securities violations. Whether accurate or not, this impression may
reflect the background and training of the men appointed to
the Commission, who usually tend to be part of the very community which they are meant to police. More emphasis on the
selection of Commissioners with more objective enforcement
outlook could dramatically improve public confidence in the
SEC's ability to make the securities laws work as they should.
In addition, Congress should give consideration to placing concurrent civil enforcement jurisdiction in the United States Attorneys' offices across the country, thereby increasing the investigative and enforcement resources available and creating
some competitive pressures to keep the SEC on its toes. Right
now, only the SEC can bring civil injunction actions to stop
securities frauds. When the SEC is shorthanded or timorous,
it means that such enforcement does not go forward. It also
means that the SEC staff leans more toward civil than criminal
sanctions, since criminal prosecutions mean that they have to
turn their cases over to someone else for handling.

The business community and the legal profession should
spend more time analyzing together the waste motion and unnecessary costs in the present handling of business disputes,
and should start looking for better alternatives. The larger
community should spend more time inquiring into inadequacies
in the enforcement of laws designed to ensure free, open competition and fair dealing. Right now we are not doing a very good
job on either front. Among the possible remedies that should

be considered to reduce unnecessary litigation expense might be a requirement for the detailed reporting, in annual reports or proxy statements to stockholders of publicly held corporations, of legal expenditures above a certain amount and economic and other factors involved in pending cases. Private owners can be expected to keep a close eye on such things, but the officers of larger corporations may be concerned about other matters. Consideration should also be given to making the SEC a party to every derivative stockholders' action to ensure that the stockholders are not hurt either by unnecessary litigation or inadequate settlements. New early-conciliation procedures should also be explored to force lawyers to discuss business disputes face-to-face before the costs and lost time get out of control.

Chapter 15

The Consumer
and the Courts

A NEW YORK CITY couple recently purchased furniture which turned out to be defective. They complained to the store. The adjuster sounded sympathetic, but bills demanding payment in full kept arriving. Meanwhile the couple was also negotiating for a home mortgage. Having no legal right to return the goods without first bringing an expensive lawsuit, the couple quietly paid the furniture bill rather than risk a poor credit rating and possible loss of their mortgage.

A Scarsdale housewife joined a health club and found that it did not live up to its advertisements. She resigned in protest and stopped making payments. Several weeks later, while being interviewed by a research assistant from the United States Attorney's Office, she learned that the health club had brought suit against her, entered a default judgment and attached her bank account. All of this had happened without the housewife receiving any court papers or notice.

These not untypical experiences help explain why consumerism is sweeping the country. Scores of witnesses have paraded before legislative hearings complaining about unfair pricing, defective merchandise, poor service, high-pressure tactics and tyrannical computers. Comparative shopping studies by student and consumer groups have focused attention on pricing abuses which discriminate against the urban poor. Such phrases as "bait-and-switch" have become part of our vocabulary. Congress and the state legislatures are continually wrestling with corrective legislative proposals. Basic to all the abuses against consumers is the disadvantaged position of the customer in the courts. We have already mentioned (Chapter 4) the special problem of the poor as debtors in the courts. This chapter deals in detail with problems that affect all consumers.

Although the Constitution guarantees all citizens equal protection under the law, a strong case can be made for the assertion that, as a practical matter, our legal and judicial system has a built-in bias that favors creditors. It is significant that many law schools still require students to take courses in "Creditors' Rights," while few schools even offer courses touching on "Debtors' Rights" except in the context of small urban-law seminars. Ironically, this weighting of legal education extends even to state bar examinations, which almost always include a substantial number of questions on creditors' rights, but seldom, if ever, on debtors' rights. Most legal textbooks also speak primarily in terms of creditors' rights and remedies. Long sections of text are devoted to the procedures for repossessing goods, actions supplementary to judgment, income executions and other techniques for collecting monies due. The same preoccupation with creditors' rights has also generated countless court rules and scores of statutes. Significantly, the anachronism of civil arrest, dating back to fifteenth-century England, is still retained in modern civil-procedure codes in many states. Not only is the balance tipped in favor of the businessman who makes full legitimate use of the legal tools available for the collection of debts, but, as a practical matter, existing statutory procedures are overwhelmingly more susceptible to abuse by unethical and unscrupulous creditors than by consumers.

The following is a brief catalog of remedies generally available to creditors. Notice how summary they are in operation, how effective they are in achieving collections and how vulnerable they leave the consumer.

Repossession of goods. The Uniform Commercial Code,

which has been enacted in most states, permits the actual seizure of collateral upon a debtor's default, without any judicial process whatsover. A few states require that the debtor be notified in writing prior to repossession; most, however, do not. Thus, for example, a harried automobile owner who withholds an installment payment because he has a legitimate grievance concerning his car's performance may wake up one morning to find that his car has been removed from his driveway by the dealer. Not only may the dealer sell the car, he may also sue the original owner for any difference between the unpaid balance and the amount realized by the resale. In such a case, the original buyer makes payments on a car he no longer owns.

Garnishment of wages. Federal and state laws authorize a judgment creditor, without any further court order, to extract a portion of a debtor's wages and apply it to the amount he owes. This remedy, variously termed "income execution" or "wage deduction procedure" in some states, is probably the most widely abused collection device in the whole arsenal of weapons against consumers, particularly when it is combined with an improperly obtained default judgment. Some states even authorize judgment creditors to obtain court orders requiring debtors to make repayments on an installment basis out of assets other than wages, subject to enforcement by the contempt power.

The threat of garnishment is one of the most powerful tools available to unscrupulous merchants. How many wage-earners would risk losing their jobs over a dispute involving a few dollars' worth of defective merchandise?

Property Levies. Another procedure subject to potential abuse by judgment creditors is the power to seize items of personal property to satisfy a judgment. A hard-bitten sheriff or marshal armed with a writ can simply march into a man's home and select whatever items seem likely to produce funds on a quick sale.

Supplementary Proceedings. The judgment creditor is generally given the broadest powers of inquiry to require from a debtor the disclosure of information about personal and family finances in the quest for property or funds that might be levied upon.

Civil Arrest. Although hedged in by increasingly strict limitations, only nine states have constitutional provisions absolutely barring the imprisonment of debtors. In nearly half the states, civil arrest is authorized in cases ranging from breach of promise and fraud to instances where a creditor alleges that the debtor is concealing property that could be used to satisfy the debt. While the United States Supreme Court has never ruled on the constitutionality of civil-arrest statutes, it is certainly questionable whether due process of law is being afforded judgment debtors in those states which place the burden on the debtor to prove that he is not wrongfully concealing property. In such circumstances it is not the creditor who must prove guilt, but the debtor who must prove that he is innocent.

The tax laws also give special consideration to creditors. A merchant who cannot collect money due him is entitled to claim a tax deduction for a bad debt, while a consumer who has been bilked by an unscrupulous vendor has no equivalent deduction available to him.

Is it not strange that we provide none of these same tools to the defrauded debtor?

Why should the seller be allowed to seize property and take it back if the purchaser defaults in payment, but the buyer have no corresponding legal right?

What meaningful affirmative remedy does a purchaser have when the seller has breached his warranty?

What can a consumer do when a serviceman never shows up to fix a defective appliance?

What can the customer do when the goods delivered are not what he ordered?

These are practical, everyday problems in our industrialized society. It is not enough to say that the consumer may assert defenses if sued by the creditor. In addition to defenses, the consumer needs counsel, a chance to be heard and effective remedies of his own. Furthermore, even existing avenues for affirmative action are often inadequate. A recent survey by the

New York City Department of Consumer Affairs indicates that upwards of one-third of the consumers who win cases in Small Claims Court are unable to satisfy their judgments because of the unwillingness of marshals and sheriffs to come to their aid.

If we really mean business about consumers' rights, we need to take a fresh look at the remedies we provide for creditors and make sure that equivalent remedies are offered debtors. Obviously, in both cases, we must make the system function properly so that these resources cannot be misused by the unscrupulous. But if the tools are to be provided at all, it must be done on an evenhanded basis. We must ensure that debtors, like creditors, are afforded effective procedural remedies and adequate legal representation to protect their rights. Just as a vendor has the option to repossess goods and resell them (then sue for damages), so the purchaser should have the option to return defective goods and be released from his obligation to pay. If the creditor can take back his goods when there has been a default in payment, then the debtor should also be free to return the goods summarily where there has been a default of an equivalent obligation by the vendor. The present distinction permitting the creditor to repossess first and then sue for damages, but requiring the purchaser to sue first for annulment of the contract before he can return defective goods is obviously discriminatory. Similar changes should be made to permit effective enforcement of judgments rendered in favor of consumers in the courts.

In virtually all cases, creditors are represented by counsel in court proceedings. Debtors usually are not. Collection attorneys have successful practices and effective office operations. Debtors' attorneys usually do not. In certain types of cases, creditors' attorneys can collect their fees from the debtor, while debtors' attorneys can collect fees only in successful actions in a very few situations prescribed by statute. Because of limited resources, public-interest law offices have not been able to advise and represent debtors in most collection cases. Although collection attorneys can afford to handle claims of small amounts because of their high volume, outside attorneys usually cannot afford to defend those same claims on a case-by-case basis, much less institute legal action to enforce their clients' rights.

There are means available for ensuring that counsel are provided to represent debtors who need help. One is the authorization of counsel fees to successful litigants in cases involving misrepresentation or breach of warranty. Pennsylvania, by way of example, has a statute that awards costs and attorney's fees to the prevailing party in cases involving retail installment contracts. This, at least, puts the consumer on an equal footing with the merchant. Another alternative is the adoption of the public defender concept, providing for a full-time lawyer and staff at the courthouse who could be consulted by debtors in cases where they are sued or seek affirmative relief. In addition, it has been proposed that the Federal Trade Commission adopt a rule making it an unfair trade practice for an installment sales contract to authorize the collection of attorney's fees for the creditor if it does not also allow attorney's fees for the debtor in the case of nonperformance on the vendor's part. At least one state has adopted this principle. In Montana, where a contract provides for the recovery of attorney's fees by one party in a lawsuit concerning such contract, state law specifically provides that the other party is equally entitled to recover such fees. Thus, in any action brought by one party to such an agreement, the prevailing party may recover reasonable attorney's fees.

Once we accept the proposition that our present creditor-oriented rights and remedies can and should be changed, there are still other aspects of the judicial process affecting consumers that also need attention. Even after the debtor is placed on an equal footing with the creditor when they get to court, we still face the problem of simply ensuring that the debtor is notified that a court suit has been instituted against him. This is not as easy as it sounds.

One of the fundamental concepts of the right to "due process" guaranteed by the Constitution is that a person must be given notice that he is being sued, and that he also must be given the opportunity to present his side of the case before a judgment can be rendered against him. In order to give the required notice, attorneys for creditors generally employ private process servers to serve summonses and other legal papers on those who are being sued. Investigations continue to show that many of these process servers, who are paid on a piecework basis, still engage in the practice known as "sewer service"—filing affidavits with the courts in which they swear that service has been made upon the named defendant when, in fact, the defendant has not been served at all. These "affidavits of service" are, in turn, used as a basis for obtaining default judgments against the defendants when they fail to appear in court to offer any defense. Recent interviews with hundreds of people against whom default judgments have been entered indicate that as many as 50 per cent never received a summons despite the fact that in each case the entry of the default judgment was preceded by the filing with the court of a sworn affidavit of service by a process server. Like the Scarsdale housewife who thought she had terminated her relationship with the local health club, many debtors who had default judgments taken against them were totally unaware of those judgments until interviewed by the investigators. More typically, defendants who have not been served first learn of a default judgment when they find that their bank accounts have been attached or their wages garnished. In 1970, an unprecedented legal action was instituted in the U. S. District Court in Manhattan against a ghetto merchant, his lawyer and fifteen process servers to bar the execution of default judgments that had been entered against customers. Investigation revealed that the merchant had obtained default judgments in nearly 98 per cent of the total actions he commenced in New York City Civil Court. The complaint alleged that by engaging in "sewer service," the merchant ensured that most of the customers who were sued would be denied their day in court and a chance to raise legitimate defenses, such as fraud or breach of warranty.

The brazenness of some process servers is underscored by cases in which they have filed affidavits of personal service even when the defendants are deceased. Recently one law firm, attempting to verify whether their legal papers were being properly served, gave nine different process servers a copy of the same summons to be served upon a defendant whom the firm knew to be dead. With only one exception, all the process servers returned sworn affidavits that personal service had been made upon the deceased defendant.

The problem of sewer service is not limited to New York City alone. Official investigations have revealed that the problem is also widespread in Los Angeles, Chicago, Boston, Detroit and the District of Columbia. Although a number of notable successes have been achieved in prosecuting fraudulent process servers, it is unrealistic to expect that such action alone will end the widespread abuse. In many states, almost anyone above the age of eighteen may serve a summons. Professional process servers generally work on a contingent-fee basis—they get paid the nominal fee only if they serve a summons, and receive absolutely no compensation if they fail. Thus, their livelihood depends on a high volume and a high rate of success. Such a system only encourages abuse.

One further area of abuse in the collection process is the use of improper threats or deception in forcing consumers to make payments, and thereby denying them their day in court. Threats by merchants and collection agencies are not unusual. From Beverly Hills to Brownsville, consumers across the nation continue to report receiving abusive and harassing phone calls at unusual hours of the day and night. Others have been threatened with imprisonment. In at least one instance, although she had already paid her bill in full, a woman was told that a marshal was coming to repossess her television set and would knock her door down if she did not let him in. Bill collectors commonly present the express or implied threat of a bad credit rating.

We need to reappraise and reexamine the present legal relationships between debtors and creditors. This is not to suggest that there should not be adequate legal remedies to ensure that a businessman will be able to obtain prompt payment for services properly rendered or credit fairly extended. What it does suggest, however, is that our legal system must provide adequate protection against overzealous and unethical creditors who abuse the legal process. Both sides must be treated with equality and impartiality. The goal, as in other areas of the law and justice, must be to strike the balance true.

Chapter 16

The Media and the Courts:
The Bark Is Bigger
Than the Bite

IN 1787, Thomas Jefferson wrote to a friend: "Were it left to me to decide whether we should have a government without newspapers, or newspapers without a government, I should not hesitate to prefer the latter." Twenty years later, Jefferson wrote to another friend that "abandoned prostitution to falsehood" by certain newspapers produced the same harm in depriving the nation of the benefits of a free press as outright suppression. Indeed, he whimsically suggested, maybe it would be better if newspaper editors divided their papers into four sections, labeled "Truths," "Probabilities," "Possibilities" and "Lies."

Does a free press have any role to play in the administration of justice? If so, what is that role, and how well is the press discharging it?

The press probably has a far heavier responsibility for maintaining adequate scrutiny over the workings of the administration of justice than it does in regard to any other field of government. Its failure to fulfill this responsibility is undoubtedly one of the principal contributing causes to the conditions which foster injustices in the system.

Unlike other branches of government, there is no built-in watchdog for the judicial establishment. Our two-party system serves as a check on the Legislative and Executive branches, but not on the courts. Presidential, gubernatorial and mayoral election campaigns provide ample opportunities for the "outs" to criticize the administration of the "ins," and for those in office to defend their record of performance. Virtually every aspect of the Executive department's program and policy is vulnerable to challenge and criticism. Scandals are seized on happily by the opposing party and hammered home to the electorate.

The same is true of campaigns for Congress and the state legislatures. The incumbent's record is subject to searching examination and critical appraisal by his adversary. He is forced to justify his votes and his failure to take action on major issues of the day. He is also forced to justify his party's position on various major legislative questions.

But the two-party system has almost totally failed in regard to the courts. Theoretically, the popular election of judges should provide the same opportunities for public appraisal of the way the job is being performed, but it does not. Political deals are worked out to guarantee bipartisan nomination of many judicial candidates to avoid political contests, something that is virtually unheard of in other offices. Even where there is a "contest," the Canons of Judicial Ethics prevent partisan debates or attacks. Judicial election campaigns are, in fact, a bore. Most voters have no idea who their judicial candidates are, and take no interest in judicial races. In many urban election districts the judicial candidates only add a long list of names to an already complicated ballot. Most voters simply vote their party preferences, with no discrimination at all between particular candidates. Many voters skip over the judicial candidates entirely. A comparison of the small number of votes cast for judicial candidates appearing on the same ballot with candidates for other offices plainly demonstrates the lack of voter interest in the process of electing judges.

The resources of the two-party system, if they were used, provide our only built-in means of focusing a spotlight on the administration of justice. Other seemingly logical substitutes—judges, lawyers, and litigants—are themselves part of the very system, each with an ax to grind and a personal interest to protect. When one of this group does have the courage to express a criticism, it is usually with such politeness and restraint that it generally goes unnoticed.

We have only one real alternative to the two-party system in exposing the weaknesses and errors of the administration of justice, and that is an alert and inquiring press. While, in the case of the Legislative and Executive branches, television and newspaper reporters can simply wait for political adversaries to provide news copy about things that are wrong and need exposure and correction, this is not so for the courts. If inquiring journalists do not become directly and aggressively involved, then the defects and injustices will go on unreported.

During the past few years, there has been a controversy between the media, the bench and the bar over the matter of pretrial publicity. A desire to protect the rights of defendants to a fair trial has caused many judges to limit access of the media to the courtroom. In most courts there is an outright prohibition against television and radio broadcasting, and the photographing of the proceedings. Lawyers and law enforcement personnel are prohibited from disclosing to the press information beyond the public record which might in any way affect the opportunity of a defendant to have a fair trial. Although many responsible segments of the media have responded to these limitations in a fair way, some belligerently maintain that the "public's right to know" takes precedence over the rights of individual defendants. This shibboleth serves as a convenient argument when it comes to questions of access to court proceedings affecting an individual defendant. Ironically, when it comes to the overall quality of justice these declarations of principle are just so much rhetoric. The public may have a right to know, but the media are not doing very much to keep the public informed.

If we are to achieve true justice in this country, it cannot be done without the deep commitment of all members of the profession of journalism to serve as the public's watchdogs over the way the courts are run. This means assigning more journalists to cover the whole judicial system. It means allocating more space and time to coverage of what is wrong with the system. And, above all, it means an intellectual commitment by all concerned to understand the judicial process and to report accurately what is going on.

Anyone who reads a daily newspaper is acutely aware of the grave deficiencies in the reporting of legal proceedings. Except for a tiny handful, most journalists betray an ignorance of how the courts work when they report on judicial proceedings. When it comes to broadcast media, the chances are that the only preparation a reporter will have had when he covers a story affecting the courts is the reading of a one-paragraph bulletin that has come over a press wire service. The impact of this journalistic ignorance on effective coverage of the judicial system is self-evident. If a reporter does not understand how the system works, he cannot possibly ask questions which will expose its weaknesses. If editors will not recruit and assign informed reporters to cover the proceedings of the courts, they cannot expect to provide the public with the critical inquiry necessary in a democracy.

It is apparent that at present the public understands the deficiencies of the judicial system far better than do the media. In 1971, *Newsweek* magazine sponsored a public opinion survey which disclosed a widespread feeling that the administration of justice has deteriorated seriously in recent years. Only 23 per cent of the adult population thought that the system was working well, compared with twice that number five years before. Reflecting particularly deep distrust of the system, 70 per cent of the blacks believed that a member of their race, once suspected of a crime, is far more likely to be convicted and sentenced than a white. An overwhelming majority of both races —84 per cent of the blacks and 77 per cent of the whites— believed that the poor are more likely to be convicted and sent to prison than those who are wealthy enough to afford their own lawyers. The following basic problems were identified as seriously affecting the quality of justice in America:

Convicted criminals are let off too easily	75%
It takes too long before accused people are brought to trial	68%
Prisons are seriously overcrowded	43%
Judges are appointed for political reasons only	39%
The ordinary person cannot afford really good lawyers	32%
There is graft and corruption among police	27%
Bail is set unfairly high for poor people	21%

The striking thing about these findings is that most of the problems are totally neglected in the nation's press and television coverage. One seldom reads an analysis of the sentences imposed on convicted criminals. There are few factual articles or documentaries about delay in the criminal court system. More often than not, the overcrowding of prisons becomes newsworthy only when there is a riot. The appointment of judges is almost never a subject for journalistic coverage unless it is tied in with some topical item about a "political deal." The availability of lawyers to serve those charged with crime is a frequent subject for bar association speeches, but virtually never for newspaper or magazine articles. Graft and corruption among the police are not frequently exposed by journalists. The question of bail is a subject for law school forums but not for press analysis. Of course these subjects do occasionally appear before the public in some context, such as a speech or legislative hearing, but almost never as a result of independent investigative journalism. The media largely disregard a category of very real problems which are so prominent in the minds of most Americans. Why?

Possibly one of the reasons is that the media are themselves part of The Establishment. Professor Hillier Krieghbaum of New York University recently pointed out that the fifty biggest newspapers in the country control 30 per cent of all daily circulation, and that the three major networks control 92 per cent of prime time for television viewing. There is no longer any true newspaper competition today. Only 37 out of the 1,511 cities which have daily newspapers have two or more competing newspapers. Over half the newspapers in the country are controlled by chains, and six feature syndicates out of a total of three hundred control 40 per cent of the feature revenues. The same people who have substantial financial investments in the media are part of the group which has a substantial stake in keeping the justice system pretty much as it is, whether they realize it or not. Judges and lawyers tend to be members of the same country clubs, college alumni associations and dinner-party groups, and it is hard to be critical of personal friends. This is not to suggest anything sinister about the personal re-lationships or the business orientation of the owners of the nation's newspaper and broadcasting industry but simply to say that in their own circles there is a tendency toward myopia when it comes to the administration of justice.

One small incident makes the point. Classified advertising is a substantial source of newspaper revenue. Not long ago a con man, recently released from prison after serving a long term, embarked on a new fraudulent scheme through the classi-fied advertising pages of a major New York newspaper. He placed a series of small ads in the "Business Opportunities" section of the paper soliciting persons who had available cash to "invest." He requested such persons to get in touch with him through a box number at the newspaper. When people wrote to the box number he would then call on them and per-suade them to part with their money in a get-rich-quick scheme which promised huge profits that never materialized. Eventually he was caught, after fleecing at least forty thousand dollars out of his victims, and was duly indicted by a Federal Grand Jury.

The Consumer Fraud Unit of the U. S. Attorney's office pre-pared a press release announcing the indictment and warning persons who respond to such ads to seek professional advice before parting with their money. Although consumer stories are usually given good coverage in New York newspapers, this par-ticular story never appeared anywhere. One must assume that the various editors in good faith concluded that there were more important news stories that day, but one cannot escape the awareness that the newspapers also had a built-in conflict of interest, since a story which disclosed that con men were able to freely use classified ads and newspaper box numbers might have an adverse impact on advertising readership and revenues. Whatever the reason, the public's "right to know" was never fulfilled, and other potential victims presumably are still scanning the classified ads trustingly looking for investment opportunities.

Even where individual editors may have a desire to improve their coverage of the administration of justice, their habits and resources make this extremely difficult. Although many leading newspapers pride themselves on expertise in foreign affairs, and take great pains in selecting their foreign correspondents, when it comes to domestic matters they tend to rely for their information on press releases, press conferences and off-the-record briefings. Lacking sufficient depth of understanding about the way complicated governmental processes work, newsmen are willing to accept the information handed out to them by official agencies as the basis for informing the public. Although there may be skepticism expressed by journalists because of a personal dislike of a particular official or administration, seldom is there an informed or knowing challenge to the contents of official press handouts. It is no wonder, therefore, that one learns from Professor Krieghbaum that the Federal Government spends twice as much each year for its official public relations as the combined news budgets of the Associated Press, United Press International and the three major television networks, plus the ten largest daily newspapers in the country.

Journalists have let themselves become unwitting prisoners of the public information officers. They depend on such officers for their stories almost every day. The result has sometimes been tragic. During the 1960's, government mimeograph machines turned out pie-in-the-sky press releases about poverty programs which seemed to promise an end to all human misery and quick prosperity for the residents of the nation's black ghettos. These official promises were published verbatim by the nation's press, creating an atmosphere of high anticipation among the intended beneficiaries. When it turned out that the

government officials were putting more effort into public relations than into implementing their programs, a reverse reaction
set in. Frustration and disappointment in the ghettos over the
failure of government officials to live up to their promises undoubtedly contributed to the bloodshed and rioting in cities
across the country. It was a tragedy for which the nation's
media must take a share of the blame. Instead of asking the
right questions, they let themselves be used as propaganda
machines.

The same is true essentially in regard to the administration
of justice. Reporters and editors depend on speeches made by
judges and bar association officials, or occasionally a congressman or law enforcement officer, for their facts, and rarely seem
able to ask searching questions themselves. When the press does
try to show initiative in writing about the system of justice and
its problems, it tends to be wrong more often than right. This is
largely the result of superficiality. In April, 1972, for example,
a leading metropolitan newspaper carried an editorial lashing
out at a proposal by a special committee of the American Bar
Association which had suggested that character-evaluation tests
be given to law students during their first year in law school,
instead of just before their admission to the bar, after they had
invested three years in legal preparation. This creative idea for
weeding out those who are unqualified for the practice of a
profession depending on trust and integrity deserved far more
than a knee-jerk reaction. The newspaper editorial, however,
espoused the position that "no democracy can set up standards
of human nature," and then incongruously said that the proper
time to judge the character of candidates for the bar is *after*
they have passed their bar examinations. What kind of circular
reasoning is that? As we have seen, there are very serious
problems in maintaining ethical standards for the legal profession. Along with many other problems in the administration
of justice, they deserve far more thorough journalistic study
and analysis than they have received to date.

Former President Harry S. Truman coined a political proverb

which has become part of the American language: "If you can't stand the heat, get out of the kitchen." He was referring primarily to the newspaper abuse that a public officeholder is subjected to while he occupies his position. Apart from its humorous note, there is a forlorn truth in Mr. Truman's observation. Although one of the most useful roles of journalism is to cut people down to size and keep officials from becoming too self-important, this function is counterproductive when it takes the form of personal vendettas. Editors and reporters are human, and indulge the same foibles as other species of mankind. Frequently they allow their subjective reactions to people in public life to influence their journalistic decisions. For example, the selection of a photograph showing a public official with his mouth open in an apparent yawn, or his eyes closed in a blink, can do a great deal of harm when selected and printed for purposes of satisfying some editor's personal malice. Most people in public life can cite news stories about themselves which they considered grossly unfair. (They will usually do so only in private, however, because they are acutely aware that public criticism of the press will lead to reprisals in which the press always has the last word.)

Public officials never enjoy reading personal attacks in the press, particularly unjust ones. They have wives and children they must face at home, and they feel concern about ridicule of their offspring by schoolmates and neighbors. Although some officeholders develop thick skins in the Truman tradition, many are just as sensitive as other, more private people. These are the officials who *do* "get out of the kitchen" because they cannot stand the unfair criticism and abuse that so often accompany public service. It would be foolish to say that sensitive people do not belong in government. Indeed, it is absolutely essential to have people with decent human feelings and reactions in public service. Without them, government would be run by overcautious bureaucrats and hard-bitten professional politicians. Self-discipline on the part of the press, to ensure that personal criticism of officeholders is fair before it is rushed into print, would be a valuable contribution to the public interest, by encouraging the persons most valuable in public service to remain there.

Recently there have been expressions of concern by media spokesmen about real and imagined restrictions on their freedom. The *Pentagon Papers* case, the *Caldwell* decision, congressional subpoenas, public speeches by Vice-President Agnew and other incidents have raised cries of "repression." While newspaper and broadcasting spokesmen have concentrated on protecting their own constitutional rights, these very same spokesmen have largely overlooked their obligations to serve the public. There are many ways they could and should be doing so. They ought to challenge press handouts from government agencies. They must begin to treat public officials fairly as human beings. They should make responsible judgments as to the timing of disclosures of official investigations. They could conduct independent inquiries of their own into governmental functions, including particularly the administration of justice. The type of dogged investigative reporting demonstrated by the *Washington Post* in the Watergate affair is the standard of journalism that should be striven for by all.

In an address before the Poor Richard Club of Philadelphia, in 1971, the director of the Television Information Office expressed despair at the various threats to freedom of the press, and once more reasserted the obligation of the press to tell the public the truth about its institutions. He declared: "I want to say quite strongly, we must allow no one to enjoin us from showing the world as it is."

Despite such bold talk, the media have not shown the problems of justice as they really are. They have rarely told the public about correction institutions, judicial delays, unfair treatment of the poor, inept judges, unethical lawyers or the many other factors contributing to the present failure of our judicial system. We can never achieve true justice in this country until the media assume their full measure of responsibility. This means that instead of sending out the uninformed reporter to cover the courts, editors should hire experienced people to do the job, or invest in educating their present staff on how the system of justice works. Recently, the New York Fair Trial-Free Press Conference arranged for a one-week special internship program for reporters which would permit them to work in a prosecutor's office and follow every stage in the handling of criminal investigations and prosecutions—all without cost. A number of newspapers and local television stations sent reporters to participate in the program, but the major television stations and some of the leading daily newspapers with national circulation did not deem it worthy of their attention.

Journalists themselves need not do all the legwork in order to maintain adequate public scrutiny of the administration of justice. Reporters can accomplish just as much by goading the appropriate congressional and legislative committees to hold public hearings into matters involving the courts that deserve special attention. The Executive branch of government can also be prodded by the media into paying more attention to criminal justice and law enforcement, and can appoint special investigators or special commissions to look into particular problems. Bar associations are not immune to press inquiry; a determined reporter, willing to make some noise about a failure to provide adequate information or explanations, can do a great deal to stimulate bar association officers and committees to give more attention to problems of injustice. Judges themselves are also proper targets for questioning about the condition of the courts. The important thing is to assign manpower to ask the right questions of the right people, and then give adequate space to the results. Action will come quickly, as it recently did when *The New York Times* published a series of articles on disparities in sentencing (triggered by a prosecutor's speech on the subject). New sentencing panels were set up in a matter of days. The elections of judges can also be used by the press as a means of improving the administration of the courts. If reporters would inquire into the performance of judges who are standing for reelection, and publish their findings, the impact would be felt not just in the ensuing elections, but also in performance by other judges, who know that they must come up for re-election themselves.

All facets of our judicial system need to be examined: the training, selection and disciplining of lawyers and judges; the mistreatment of the poor; the mishandling of crimes of violence; the inability to deter professional criminals; delay and over-crowding in the courts; inept, unfair law enforcement; the failure of corrections; ineffective response to antisocial conduct; instances of governmental harassment of individual citizens; mistaken approaches to juvenile problems; waste and delay in automobile-accident claims; inadequate policing of business abuses; oppression of consumers. Why have these things been allowed to occur? What can be done about them? This is what the public has a right to know. Being the public's watchdog is the undone job of the media.

Chapter 17

"What are you going to do about it?"

SHORTLY after 11 P.M. on April 30, 1971, a tall, twenty-three-year-old black man walked into a grocery store in a white section of Detroit, Michigan, drew a revolver out of his coat pocket, pointed it toward the store manager and demanded that he hand over the money in the cash register. The manager reached under the counter, pulled out his own gun and emptied it in the direction of the intruder, who fell wounded to the floor. Four and a half hours later the young black man died in Detroit General Hospital from the effects of five gunshot wounds.

The case appeared to be just another violent crime in a city where over thirteen thousand armed robberies had occurred during the preceding year, but there was one significant difference. When the detectives went through the dead man's wallet looking for identification, they found a small white card bearing the inscription "Congressional Medal of Honor Society, United States of America." The armed robber was a war hero.

Sergeant Dwight Johnson was an illegitimate son of an unknown father, conceived while his mother was still a teenager. He grew up in a public housing project in the poor black district of Detroit. He was drafted into the Army and sent to Vietnam. One morning, when his platoon of four M-48 tanks was racing down a road toward Dakto, in the Central Highlands near the

Cambodian border and the Ho Chi Minh Trail, the tanks were ambushed by North Vietnamese soldiers. Two of the tanks were knocked out by Communist rockets. Sergeant Johnson had just been reassigned from one of the tanks to another, and the tank he had left the day before was one of those hit. As it burst into flames, Johnson tried to help his buddies. He had succeeded in pulling one of them out of the hatch when the tank's ammunition supply exploded and killed everyone else inside. Suddenly, something snapped inside Sergeant Johnson, and for the next thirty minutes he went berserk, killing every Vietnamese soldier he could find, first with a .45-caliber pistol, then with a submachine gun, and finally, when he ran out of ammunition, with the stock of his rifle.

When Sergeant Johnson returned to Detroit after his tour of duty, he did not discuss the incident near Dakto with anyone. Like other black veterans, he struggled to find work but was never able to get a job. Then one day he received a call from a colonel advising him that he had been awarded the Congressional Medal of Honor and inviting him to go to Washington. President Johnson presented the medal to Sergeant Johnson along with five other Vietnam veterans at a ceremony in the White House. After Johnson returned home to Detroit as the only living Medal of Honor winner in Michigan, he was suddenly in great demand. Job offers poured in from many large companies, who saw the public-relations advantage of having him on their payroll, but Johnson accepted instead an offer to return to the Army as a recruiter. Thereafter he was wined and dined at a series of luncheons and dinners, supplied with a Thunderbird by the Ford Motor Company and showered with gifts and credit. He bought a house with a sixteen-thousand-dollar mortgage.

After the initial wave of publicity had receded, Sergeant Johnson came face to face with reality in the form of unpaid bills and demands upon him which his own ghetto background had not equipped him to handle. He began to experience stomach pains and was sent to Valley Forge Army Hospital for tests.

The medical examination disclosed nothing physically wrong, but the psychiatrist's study produced the following preliminary diagnosis: "Depression caused by post-Vietnam adjustment problem."

Sergeant Johnson continued to be haunted by money worries and nightmares about his Vietnam experience. He thought about his dead buddies and wondered why he should have been spared. Then, when he heard the news that Lt. William L. Calley, Jr., had been convicted of murdering Vietnamese civilians, Sergeant Johnson walked out of the Army hospital and went home to Detroit. He avoided calls from the Army authorities and the bill collectors. Foreclosure proceedings were started on the mortgage on his home. He fell behind in his payments on a credit-union loan. The Ford Motor Company recalled his car, and a secondhand vehicle he bought in its place required brake repairs. His young wife entered the hospital for a minor operation, and he was pressed by the hospital for a cash deposit. On April 30, Sergeant Johnson visited his wife in the hospital and she told him that the hospital was again pressing for the cash deposit. He left at 5:30 P.M. and promised to return later that evening. With help from a friend who owned a car, Johnson went to another section of the city, saying that he was going to collect some money that someone owed him. He left the car and walked the distance to the grocery store. There his attempted holdup resulted in his death.

A TIME FOR REEXAMINATION

Today, the universal reaction to crimes of violence, such as armed robbery of a grocery store, is that they must be dealt with swiftly and severely. Prison sentences are generally very stiff. No one seems to believe that rehabilitation is possible, so little effort is made. Our whole attitude is blinded by emotion and unreasoned reaction. As the story of Sergeant Johnson makes plain, however, there can be many explanations for the commission of violent crimes, some of which can provide the key for treatment and rehabilitation. The problem is that we have not tried.

In the December, 1971, issue of *Federal Probation*, a professional journal published by the Probation Division of the Administrative Office of the United States Courts, a faculty member from the Centre of Criminology in Ottawa, Canada, discussed the taboo against violent offenders and stated that most decisions affecting their sentencing and treatment are based on bias, fear and ignorance. While making it clear that he was not proposing a general policy of leniency toward those who commit crimes of violence, since many of these persons are so dangerous that they pose a continuing threat to society, the criminologist suggested exploring the use of an indeterminate period of imprisonment as a possible recourse, which would lead to the eventual return of the offenders to society under proper supervision and precaution. He concluded:

> There is no one simple explanation for violent crime nor will any one typology satisfactorily characterize all such offenders. Rehabilitation of such offenders is, therefore, a complex matter. In striving to act on the basis of our current knowledge, and to be continually aware of the need to reappraise our values and attitudes, society must continue its efforts to rehabilitate all its offenders, including the violent offender.

This flicker of enlightenment is encouraging, but hardly revolutionary. How much we still have to learn about ourselves and our own slow evolution from the aggressive animal world. How much we have to learn from anthropologists like Robert Ardrey, who wrote in *African Genesis* that "Man is a predator whose natural instinct is to kill with a weapon."

Given man's underlying instincts, it is indeed ironic that we should react so emotionally and so harshly against the offender who commits a crime when he is armed with a handgun, while at the same time we exhibit almost equal emotion in our resistance to any legislative efforts to control the sale and distribution of handguns, and are so lenient toward those who sell or possess guns in violation of such laws as do exist.

Our approach to violent crime is only one of the basic tenets that must be challenged if we are to put our system of justice in order. Our overall approach to sentencing and correction needs reorientation. We have created a monster by imposing on judges the task of determining both the best course for rehabilitating an offender and the best course for deterring others from committing similar crimes. We should give rehabilitation and retraining experts the job of deciding what form of treatment might best salvage a particular offender, as well as the length of time needed. These officials, rather than the judge, should have the responsibility of classifying the offender for the proper kind of treatment and supervision, preparing him for return to society and deciding when he is ready for release (within limits set by the court). Much heavier emphasis should also be placed on pretrial diversion of offenders immediately following arrest, whenever rehabilitation professionals find that this would be the optimum means for achieving productive results, and the defendant, his counsel and the prosecuting attorney all consent. Those who supervise treatment and rehabilitation should include qualified ex-offenders and others who can relate to the men and women who are assigned to them, including a substantial percentage from similar ethnic, community and economic backgrounds.

Part of any reappraisal of correction techniques should include a fresh look at the use made of the fingerprint record taken at the time of arrest. Ordinarily this record is used to prepare a "rap sheet" listing prior arrests for criminal violations. Serious consideration should be given to using fingerprints to trigger a computer printout of accumulated information on the violator's background which would be helpful in prompt assessment of the possibilities of pretrial diversion or other ways of achieving effective treatment or rehabilitation. Such data might include background material on home environment, family history, school and employment records, details of prior treatment for personality disorders, results of any earlier testing, diagnosis and efforts at rehabilitation, and results.

One obvious benefit from automatically turning convicted defendants over to rehabilitation specialists is that it would no longer be necessary to prepare the time-consuming pre-sentence reports for use by the judge, thereby eliminating as much as six to ten weeks of delay in the criminal justice process. Such an approach would also make possible merger of the separate functions of the probation officer, correction officer and parole officer, all of whom presently operate at various steps in the process, into a single professional group responsible for salvaging the individual offender from the moment he is first arrested until he finally returns to society. The process of planning for rehabilitation should begin immediately upon arrest and get under way as soon as possible.

With the responsibility for rehabilitation removed from the trial judge, his principal function would be to ensure due process in the adjudication function. He should represent the public interest in seeing to it that each criminal case is processed without unnecessary delay. After a defendant is adjudicated guilty of an offense, the trial judge's job might properly include determining whether any reparations are necessary to the victims of the crime; taking steps to be sure that the defendant has not profited by his criminal conduct; and deciding whether there are ways in which the offender can make amends to society itself for his violations, such as by supplying information and testimony, where appropriate, against others engaged with him in criminal conduct. The judge must also decide what penalty is reeded to deter others from committing similar violations.

In making decisions about deterrence, it must be borne in mind that a prison sentence is not the only option. Under Indian law, jails were totally unknown and punishment was meted out in the form of public whippings. This is not to suggest that corporal punishment is a proper penalty in a "civilized" society, but simply that jail is not necessarily the only remedy. In Bulgaria, one form of punishment is deportation. In France, a convicted criminal may be exiled from certain sections of the country. Fines which are meaningful in terms of the defendant's true net worth can constitute an effective deterrent as well. A wider range of options should be developed.

GOALS FOR CRIMINAL JUSTICE

If one were to try to catalog the basic changes that are needed in our criminal justice system, the result might look like this:

1. Eliminate inappropriate use of criminal sanctions:

(a) develop new remedies for "victimless" crimes;

(b) authorize District Attorneys to use civil remedies whenever appropriate;

(c) establish nationwide and statewide coordination of prosecution policies and allocation of law enforcement resources.

2. Develop better alternatives to traditional criminal prosecution:

(a) establish procedure for personality and background testing immediately upon arrest;

(b) eliminate bail and determine pretrial release on basis of (1) risk of flight and (2) dangerous personality disorders, as indicated by personality and background evaluation testing;

(c) offer immediate voluntary enrollment in supervised treatment, counseling, education and employment programs in lieu of prosecution to all suitably qualified candidates;

(d) ensure adequate coordination of psychiatric testing and treatment for defendants with personality disorders; maintain personality profile data along with fingerprint records for quick reference.

3. Guarantee fairness in court procedures for those who must stand trial:

(a) implement commonsense speedy trial and speedy appeal rules;

(b) establish procedures for eliminating or strictly supervising plea bargaining;

(c) use court-appointed panel for all medical and psychiatric testing of defendants;

(d) equalize access of defendants to qualified counsel.

4. Improve system of corrections:

(a) establish permanent commission with lay and professional membership to fix uniform sentencing policies and correct sentencing disparities;

(b) reorient corrections policy and management to separate rehabilitation from custodial functions, and ensure adequate funding and staffing for both;

(c) eliminate prison "underworld" through more structured use of inmate abilities and motivations;

(d) replace parole system with indeterminate release program based on inmate achievements and evaluations.

GOALS FOR CIVIL JUSTICE

A similar catalog of changes needed in our civil justice system is the following:

1. Automobile accident cases should be removed from the courts as much as possible, while still protecting the seriously injured claimant.

2. Consumers and individual citizens of moderate means should have quality legal assistance readily available to advise them on their rights and remedies and to protect them in court.

3. Process-serving must be more effectively policed to ensure the integrity of the judicial process.

4. In business cases involving public corporations, full disclosure of substantial litigation expense should be made to stockholders. The SEC should be made a party to all derivative stockholder actions. Early conciliation efforts in business disputes should be mandatory.

5. The courts should be given a larger role in using civil alternatives to criminal prosecutions, with power to order censure, penalties, injunctions, restitution and damages, and civil commitment for treatment.

GOALS FOR SOCIAL JUSTICE

Our legal system is intimately intertwined with many citizen rights in the larger community. The following catalog of needed changes could help achieve broader justice in our contemporary society:

1. The courts should expand their activist role in social-problem areas involving new legal rights and remedies. This would include the areas of equal job opportunities, protection of consumers, welfare and poverty programs, health services, public school funding, housing, care for the aged.

2. The rights of the individual citizen in dealing with government and the courts should be strengthened through procedural changes and access to good legal assistance.

3. Law enforcement resources should be strengthened to deal more effectively with organized crime and white-collar crime, which prey on large numbers of victims. Local police forces should be coordinated on a regional basis and local prosecutors should be selected on a nonpartisan merit basis.

4. Ex-offenders should have the same rights as first-class citizens, which should be limited only when justified on a clear factual showing. Those with arrest records only should be treated as innocent until proven otherwise.

5. Family life should be affirmatively supported through such government aid as tax relief, family planning and counseling, recreation and school programs, and welfare, health and other social services. Juvenile facilities, in particular, should receive priority attention to aid them in nurturing personality development rather than providing merely punitive restraints.

6. Constitutional rights should be guaranteed through commonsense application of disciplinary sanctions against those who violate them, rather than treated as academic exercises which aid the corrupt and harm the public interest.

7. The media should assume a direct and active role in exposing the causes of injustice in our legal system, pointing out

problems concerning corrections, delays, unfairness, inept judges, unethical lawyers and any other matters that need public scrutiny and attention.

THE MACHINERY OF JUSTICE

In terms of human experience, there is nothing sacrosant about the American judicial structure. In China, "People's Conciliation Committees" are set up to settle disputes, instead of using the formal court process. In England, a jury which is unable to reach a unanimous verdict after two hours may bring in a majority verdict of at least ten out of twelve. Also in England, the main question in a criminal appeal is whether a reasonable jury with the same evidence before it might have failed to convict, rather than whether there were any technical violations of rules of evidence or procedure. In Finland, the trial judge makes the original decision and the trial jury then reviews it. Only if the members of the jury unanimously disagree with the judge is his decision overruled. In Guatemala, judges, along with other public officials, are required to file a full accounting of their private property and income when they enter office, and also when they leave.

All Hungarian courts of first instance consist of one professional judge and two "people's assessors." The judges of Irish higher courts are appointed only from among barristers specially trained and admitted to practice in court. Mexican judges are appointed by the Congress for six-year terms. Most serious crimes in the Netherlands are tried by three-judge courts. A "Conciliation Council" is set up in each Norwegian community, consisting of three persons elected by a district council, and all civil cases must first be brought before the Conciliation Council for mediation before they can be heard in court. Norway also provides for lay judges on all courts except the Supreme Court, and in order to insure equality of legal representation the government pays both the prosecutor and defense counsel in criminal cases. In Peru, the judges of the highest court are selected by Congress from lists submitted by the Executive; on the trial level, judges are selected by the Executive from candidates proposed by the other members of the court.

All Philippine judges are appointed by the President with the consent of a "Commission on Appointments." Minor criminal cases in Sweden are tried before a jury of three members; in major criminal cases, the trial judge makes the initial decision, which is controlling unless the entire jury of seven to nine members disagrees with him. Swiss jurors are elected by the people to sit in the assize courts. In Russia, most civil and criminal cases are heard in people's courts, which consist of a judge, who is elected for a five-year term, and two assessors, who are elected for two-year terms and called on a rotating basis to hear cases for two weeks each year.

These examples are cited to show that our form of judicial machinery is not universal. What we should be doing is examining whether any of these other countries have particular procedures which work better than ours, and adopting the most usable ideas. We are not so endowed with special wisdom that we can afford to be rigid. Indeed, a continuing quest for useful experience elsewhere should be part of a regular process of assessing our system of justice. Such studies as have been made tend to concentrate on the practice in England because of the common origins of our system of justice. But we have reached a stage in world communications which allows us no excuse for remaining ignorant of, or disregarding, the experience of other nations in trying to provide fair and impartial justice.

THE QUALITY OF LAWYERS AND JUDGES

Chief Justice Burger recently observed that if John Adams, Alexander Hamilton and Thomas Jefferson were brought back today, they could walk into court in Washington, D.C., or St. Paul, or San Francisco and try a case with only a short briefing on recent changes in procedure and case law. That is a pretty sad commentary on how slowly we have moved in modernizing our system of justice. The same must also be said for the methods we use in selecting lawyers and judges.

The training and admission of lawyers to practice in America still follows the original colonial concept of a small, self-disciplined legal fraternity. Yet the law profession is no longer small, and it is certainly not able to discipline itself. One result is that there has been a sharp deterioration in the public's view of the attorney. In a recent survey conducted for the Joint Commission on Correctional Manpower and Training, respondents were asked to rate their confidence in eleven different occupations. The ratings ran as follows: clergy, 77 per cent; doctors, 74 per cent; scientists, 67 per cent; schoolteachers, 62 per cent; college teachers, 57 per cent; correction workers, 57 per cent; law enforcement officials, 55 per cent; social workers, 54 per cent; psychiatrists, 50 per cent; businessmen, 43 per cent; lawyers, 42 per cent. It is not without significance that lawyers ended up at the bottom of the list. A similar public attitude toward judges was reflected in a *Newsweek* poll in which 40 per cent of the respondents blamed lenient judges for the increase in crime, and 39 per cent said that one of the problems seriously affecting the quality of justice in America is that judges are appointed for political reasons only. This substantial lack of confidence in attorneys and judges cannot be disregarded. Unless the public has confidence in those who run the judicial system, they are not going to have confidence in the system itself.

One possible way of raising the integrity level of lawyers who appear in the courts would be through the creation of a small specialized body of attorneys to do trial work. This is the system of solicitors and barristers which is at the heart of the English system of justice, and which largely explains the public confidence in that system. Solicitors work directly with clients and provide office service and advice. Barristers, who do the court work, are retained by solicitors, never by clients directly. Those who may practice in court are few in number, and are assigned equally to represent both the government and the accused in the criminal courts, thus ensuring evenhanded professional representation. The smallness of the group, and the closeness of training and supervision, make it possible to maintain the highest professional standards and discipline, both because the barristers know they must deal with each other on a regular basis and because the cohesiveness of the bar makes it possible to keep track of what each lawyer is doing. In America, however, there is a philosophical obstacle to adopting the barrister concept, since it involves the creation of a special professional elite, which runs counter to our democratic traditions. Moreover, the number of lawyers available to represent persons of limited means is already so small that it is hard to visualize an even more restricted professional group that would handle all courtroom work. Possibly the American equivalent to the British approach might include a regulated body of trained lay personnel to perform certain quasi-legal functions and a highly professionalized group to perform more complex legal tasks, including courtroom work.

Special attention should be paid to the adequacy of training in our law schools, particularly in basic skills, tradition, ethics and fiduciary obligation. Special attention must also be given to the role of the criminal lawyer.

Another basic need is to strengthen the disciplinary machinery for lawyers. If nature takes its course, we will continue to witness a rapid expansion of attorneys in this country and the erosion of character and integrity tests as a condition of admission to the bar. Without the inherent checks of a small bar and a strictly regulated process of education and admission, professional standards will inevitably be weakened still further. With the growing depersonalization of the legal profession, new techniques for control and discipline must therefore be found. It is not enough to leave the process up to bar association groups, which depend heavily on voluntary complaints and volunteer efforts by lawyers to serve on grievance committees. Instead, a more permanent, adequately staffed, full-time enforcement agency must be created, with responsibility for initiating investigations of possible misconduct rather than simply sitting back and waiting for complaints to come in. Such a disciplinary body should be at least quasi-public in nature, since the public interest is so much involved in the work of lawyers and courts. Presumably the job would fall to some administrative agency, such as the state licensing body. A public disciplinary agency to supervise lawyers need not have exclusive jurisdiction, and complaints could also still be heard by bar associations.

Our method of picking judges is catch-as-catch-can. Whether appointive or elective, too much emphasis is on rewarding the party faithful, and not enough on finding men who have the professional qualifications, temperament and personality to make topflight judges. An obvious direction for reform is developing a career service for the judiciary, with judges started off on the judicial ladder immediately upon graduation from law school or special professional graduate training, and promotion from the lower courts to the higher courts based on merit and performance. This system appears to have worked well in many countries. Some procedure should also exist for adding judges from the trial bar, keeping in mind that there are many instances where the development of judicial talents and interest may not come until after a lawyer has been in practice for some years.

Barring such a sweeping change in our approach to developing judicial manpower, a concentrated effort must be made to improve the existing methods of judicial selection. Partisan election of judges is a totally unworkable anachronism in a large metropolitan area, and should be abolished unless it can be effectively hemmed in with checks on the nominating process. All the present procedure does is place in the hands of the political leaders of the dominant party the power of appointment and, hence, the power of rewarding those who have been politically loyal. Experience indicates that the most workable system should include elements of prescreening by a qualified committee combined with the procedure followed in the Federal courts, under which the candidate is appointed by the chief executive, subject to public hearings and confirmation by the legislative body. The public hearing feature serves as an *in terrorem* obstacle for unqualified candidates, who generally shy away from the public embarrassment of a possible challenge. By occasional turndowns of unqualified candidates, the appointing official is pretty well forced to come up with qualified candidates to avoid embarrassment himself. Hand in hand with such improvements in the selection process must also come new disciplinary machinery for judges. A quasi-public agency with power to initiate investigations is an absolute necessity.

The key to all of these efforts to improve the quality of justice is improving the quality of the attorneys and judges who make the system work. Arthur T. Vanderbilt, former Dean of New York University Law School, later Chief Justice of the State of New Jersey and an active reformer in the field of judicial administration, used to say, "Judicial reform is no sport for the shortwinded." Experience has taught us that Justice Vanderbilt's observation was an understatement. Despite well-intentioned efforts by lawyers' groups, judges and bar associations, most of which have been woefully inadequate to the task, judicial reform has not caught up with the needs of present-day society. Public confidence in our system of justice is at low ebb. Evidences of unfairness and injustice continue to multiply. We cannot control crime or the criminal. Justice in its broadest sense is in trouble. Improving the quality of justice is no job to be left just to attorneys and judges. It is the concern of every citizen, and of every public official. Possibly the most important engine of reform that can help achieve justice in our time is a free press willing and able to take on the responsibility of exposing wrongs and helping to produce right methods and results. Until the press, the public and government officials—along with the lawyers and the judges—meet their responsibilities, full and equal justice will not become a reality in America.

*   *   *

Thomas Nast's most famous cartoon of Boss Tweed, the political leader who corrupted state and local government and the courts in New York during the 1860's and 1870's, depicts

Tweed as a Roman emperor, looking on while his Tammany Tiger attacks the female figure of The Republic. The cartoon is captioned "The Tammany Tiger Loose?" After the caption is quoted the defiant response of Tweed when first confronted with evidence of his thefts from the City treasury: "What are you going to do about it?" In Tweed's case, a newspaper crusade, plus a group of angry lawyers, plus an aroused electorate provided the combination to bring an end to the worst municipal scandal in the nation's history. The press, the bar and the people together did something about it. Today, a hundred years later, as we look in dismay at the injustices in our judicial system, we can well turn to each other and ask once again, "What are you going to *do* about it?"

Index